2003

Michael Z. Brooke
William R. Mills

New Product Development
Successful Innovation in the Marketplace

Pre-publication
REVIEW

New Product Development
Successful Innovation in the Marketplace

INTERNATIONAL BUSINESS PRESS®
Erdener Kaynak, PhD
Executive Editor

New Product Development
Successful Innovation in the Marketplace

Michael Z. Brooke
William R. Mills

International Business Press®
An Imprint of The Haworth Press, Inc.
New York • London • Oxford

Published by

International Business Press®, an imprint of The Haworth Press, Inc., 10 Alice Street, Binghamton, NY 13904-1580.

Cover design by Jennifer M. Gaska.

Library of Congress Cataloging-in-Publication Data

Brooke, Michael Z.
New product development : successful innovation in the marketplace / Michael Z. Brooke, William R. Mills.
p. cm.
Includes bibliographical references and index.
ISBN 0-7890-1566-8 (alk. paper)—ISBN 0-7890-1567-6 (soft)
1. New products. I. Mills, William R. II. Title.

HF5415.153 .B76 2002
658.5'75—dc21
2002068763

CONTENTS

Foreword

Innovation in business, essential for profitable growth, is a tough and exacting discipline. I therefore commend this book to all present and future captains of industry.

It covers every aspect of new product development: spotting opportunities, forward planning, budgeting, design, research, avoiding pitfalls, coping with setbacks, ensuring market acceptance, and effective launch. It confirms the old adage "innovation is 10 percent inspiration and 90 percent perspiration."

It has been written by a professional author, Michael Brooke, and an experienced businessman, Bill Mills. My colleagues and I have made good use of their previous book, *The Visionary Executive*. They have provided an executive summary, convenient for selecting subjects of immediate concern. By reading the entire book, however, one learns how to succeed in the area of business in which achievement is so vital, yet where so many enterprises fail.

Hugh D. Facey, MBE
Executive Chairman, Gripple Ltd.

ABOUT THE AUTHORS

Michael Z. Brooke (born 1921 and a wartime coal miner) was Senior Lecturer in Management Sciences and Director of the International Business Unit at the University of Manchester Institute of Science and Technology. He has held visiting professorships in both the United States and Canada; he has also conducted numerous seminars in both countries. A professional author, this book is his 25th.

William R. Mills (born 1919 and a wartime Major in the Parachute Regiment) has had a long career at senior levels in business including serving as Vice-President, Europe, for Stanley Works. After his retirement from his last appointment in business—Chairman of Bassett Foods—he set up a consultancy. His experience with clients was the inspiration for this book.

Preface

This book demonstrates how innovation, far from being a staff function, is a dynamic line-management task. Innovation calls for the same aggressive thrust as marketing and sales and every officer of the company has a share in its responsibility.

Successful innovation is fraught with difficulty. In the field of medicine and surgery, the funds available from governments around the world cannot finance the huge volume of new medical discoveries and improvements in surgical techniques. In the area of information technology and other "high-tech" products, the race for new product development saps up profitability and prevents the conservation of financial reserves. Small, medium-size, and even large companies constantly face massive problems in achieving successful innovation. These problems include inaccurate budgeting, costs exceeding budgets, faulty market and technical research findings, flaws in design, lack of durable materials, unforeseen customer rejection through lack of consumer trials, leakage of plans to competitors, failure by outside suppliers, missed opportunities for cooperation with outside specialists, uncoordinated research and development staff, ineffective leadership, and many more. This book shows how to avoid and deal with all of these problems.

First, I express my warmest thanks to co-author Dr. Michael Brooke for inviting me to share in the writing of this book.

Second, I express my gratitude to so many friends and colleagues who have helped: Alan Smith, Chairman of Insight Monitoring Ltd.; Brian Shawcross, Principal of Almec Design Services Ltd.; Dr. Michael Cole, Retired Chairman of Genevac Ltd.; Andrew Siddall, Chief Executive of Siddall and Hilton Group; Christopher Redfearn, Managing Director, Redfearn's Wire Products Ltd.; David Partridge, Managing Director and Brian Baxter, Finance Director, Carbolite Furnaces Ltd.; Roger Bowers, Retired Chairman and Graham Keefe, Production Director, Bowers Metrology; Tony Lisanti, Group Chief

Executive, Spear and Jackson International Plc.; Robert Dangerfield, Public Relations Manager, British Gas Plc.; Bruce Everiss, Head of Communications, Codemasters; Michael Wilson, Chief Executive, St. James's Place Capital Plc.; Placid P Gonzales, Partner, St. James's Place Partnership; Tony Massarella, Marketing Director, Zimmer Ltd.; David Hirst OBE, Engineering Director, GQ Parachutes Ltd.; David Wright, Managing Director, G. R. Wright and Son Ltd.; Nigel Tomlinson, Chief Executive, Sheffield Chamber of Commerce and Industry; Michael Corner OBE, Principal, Corner Communications; Gina Consalvo, Account Coordinator, Mullen PR, Wenham, Massachusetts.

Third, I am grateful to Liz Hickson, who has coped with all my drafts and to my wife, Doris, for her help in composing them.

William R. Mills

We offer this book to readers in the hope that it will deepen under-standing of corporate strategy, its formulation and implementation.

My colleague, Bill Mills, who suggested this subject, tells me that, in his long experience, new product strategy is a crucial weakness in numbers of businesses. Bill's insight set us on a trail which has now produced this book which we hope will do justice to the many sides of this subject.

I am grateful to Bill for suggesting the idea for this book. I am also most grateful to Hugh Facey for producing such an inspired foreword which expresses the purpose of the book in a nutshell. As always, my thanks to my very conscientious and patient assistant, Liz Hickson, who has keyed and rekeyed the entire manuscript many times while drawing my attention to weaknesses such as duplications.

Any reader who has questions about the material in this book may phone me at +44 (0)161-746-8140. I include my phone number in the preface of all my books to ease communication, but be assured that neither my colleague nor I will attempt to sell you our services (heaven forbid!). If, by any chance, the question requires knowledge that we do not have, we *may* refer you to an independent expert.

Have a good day and very good reading.

Michael Z. Brooke

Using This Book

Readers will use this book for two different purposes: dipping and reading. Most will be dippers. Let us look at the two in more detail.

Readers

We hope you will find this book as much fun to read as we have found it to write. It contains some fascinating stories of the ways some firms have grappled with the problems of innovation on new product development. No one claims that a management book competes with fiction for a bedside read, but this one is designed to compete with any book on the market for reading on the commuter train, the plane, or the doctor's waiting room. Nevertheless, some readers will benefit greatly from reading the book from beginning to end. With this in mind, *New Product Development* has been designed to fit the modern briefcase, and is also broken up into short chapters and self-contained parts that make the reading easier.

Dippers

Most of you will treat this book as a pocket (or briefcase!) consultant, always at your side when you need help to crack a problem or to exploit an opportunity. To make your dipping easier, the book is divided into four parts, each of which identifies an issue which is focused by the chapter headings. This convenient arrangement is supported by a subject index for which we have selected a limited number of entries for each topic. This index does not set out to dazzle readers with an array of page numbers; it concentrates on helping readers to find answers to the questions they are likely to ask.

For instance, if the reader is looking to establish a center of excellence in some service, product, or technique, consult Part III. Chapters address crucial issues which are needed in plotting the center of excellence. These are listed in the chapter titles: Chapter 8, "Staffing";

Chapter 9, "In-House or Contracting Out?"; Chapter 10, "Design"; and Chapter 11, "Technical Research." Choose the one which matters right now. Then locate the industry sector in subsequent chapters. These include Chapter 12, "High Tech"; Chapter 13, "New Products by Branding: Basic Industries"; Chapter 14, "Services"; and Chapter 15, "Market Research." This division of chapters spotlights an easily overlooked fact—that centers of excellence can develop in any business sector, no matter how routine.

Part III ends with two chapters introducing other issues for discussion. Taking one from a recent celebrated antitrust case in the United States and a headline in *The Economist*, we have subtitled the chapter on relations between companies and governments "Poor Mr. Gates," after which the section ends with Chapter 17, "Failures," a subject not to be ignored in a book like this.

Both readers and dippers may well have come to this book as a result of attending a seminar. The knowledge and inspiration gained there can be built on by reading these pages; both authors have frequently attended seminars, as speakers and as participants, and we know very well how demand for follow-up literature arises.

Executive Summary

The basics of each chapter are discussed chapter by chapter. A few notes at the end of each chapter briefly outline the main lessons. This "summary" is an extended version of those points. The summary may be skimmed to identify chapters for further information.

Chapter 1. Innovation: A Relentless Thrust

The first chapter tells the reader what to expect, the body of knowledge on the search for new products: the factors that produce success and profit—ideas, strategies, and tactics put forward in each chapter.

Chapter 2. Making Innovations Happen

This chapter is one of two that discusses the importance of people, the need for vision in the innovation process; Chapter 8 also looks at the creation of an innovation team along with its leader and members ("the members of the team will be busy executives who have built up reputations in their existing jobs"). An imaginary project team discussion, led by the chairman, is included. The questions that members of the team should be asking themselves and one another are specified. This chapter states that "a system needs to be in place within which the new product leaders, groups, and committees can be developed and can work efficiently." This is an important theme of this book.

Chapter 3. Success

- The opportunity for meeting an unsatisfied demand (Can we see a substantial gap in the market to be filled?)
- Matches contemporary market scene (Have we got our timing right?)

- Uses more effectively a company's existing resources (staff, cash, reputation. Is there any other way that we could use our time, people, and money?)
- Carefully-thought-out design that picks up and promotes a company's existing image (Can we identify the design advantages or disadvantages compared with existing and competitive products?) See also Chapter 10.
- Avoid backing a shrinking industry (But check: is it *really* shrinking or redirecting itself?)
- Probability of achieving a viable market share (Can we forecast a market share to make the project worthwhile?)
- Watching life cycles of existing products and projects
- Opening up new markets (What new markets do we foresee?)
- Price: achieving a profitable price (This *may* involve cost reduction measures. What price can we obtain to sell at the volume we plan?)
- Return on investment (The new product must have an estimated return higher than existing projects. Do we foresee the company's success criteria being met?)
- Ability to manage new markets (Do we actually realize what market changes we have to meet? Can we cope with them?)
- Obsolescence (Examine exact facts and chances. What products will be obsolete and what effect will this have on corporate profitability?)
- Ability to use new materials (What advantage can we take from new materials, value engineering, and other quality or cost reducing measures?)
- Ability to use market research effectively. (Have we researched the market in sufficient depth?) This does not have to be an expensive process. Use simpler methods that may be adequate and do not take up more resources than we can commit.
- Speed of entry (Can we be first into the market? Are there advantages in being first or is it better to wait?)
- International (What is the potential for establishment and exploitation in our overseas markets?)
- Targets achieved (Are our targets realistic, and are we confident of hitting them?)

And—finally—a checklist of our main issues:

- Types of new (innovative) ideas—close to existing or more remote
- Sources of ideas (see also Chapter 5)

  —From inside the company: managers, sales representatives, designers, engineers, shop floor workers
  —From outside the company: customers, competitors, publications, and guided conversations

Never forget that ideas need a stimulus, a constant search for sources which need to be handled so that they are on tap. Sources need to be treated in ways that will not cause them to dry up. The successful manager easily stops progress by discouraging new developments. "Not invented here" is a disease, not a myth.

Chapter 4. Hitting the Ground Running

The basic message of this follows from its title: the importance of timing. The innovator must keep ahead of the competitors, unless the product is totally new in which case it—the innovator company—may leave it to a competitor to prepare the market and to face the initial losses.

The Fine Judgment. This is a fine judgment and the company needs to assess carefully the advantages and disadvantages of the proposed tactic. Some procedures will be required to make the necessary assessments and to judge a feasible speed.

Size of Company. Great care is taken in this chapter to make it relevant to companies of varying sizes, although the small one-person business will obviously not be setting up processes—committees or working parties—to discuss issues which are all in the "one person's" head!

Chapter 5. Ideas, Ideas, Ideas

This chapter lists the sources of ideas available to a company. From inside the company: members of project groups and other employees, research and development departments. From outside the company: customer monitoring of markets and especially of competitors, management seminars, libraries, museums. Between the inside and the outside: the market research department feeding in the results of their investigations.

Also identified are the criteria for judging proposals. A final paragraph headed "environmentally friendly products" points out the world markets that are growing for products regarded as friendly to the environment.

Chapter 6. Product Development: Corporate Strategy

This chapter makes the crucial point that the new product development must fit the outline devised in the statement of corporate strategy. Obvious, you might think, but often overlooked when a corporate strategy which has taken a long time to devise is sabotaged by an impulsive move into contradictory products. (Example: the strategy must not be allowed to become a straightjacket and must permit the effects of lateral thinking.)

Chapter 7. Centers of Excellence

This chapter provides a series of examples of companies from both the manufacturing and the service sectors that illustrate the following principles.

- The view that customer service is an important product for a service company.
- The need for intensive research, way beyond the state of the art, for a technical service firm.
- The need for adequate, usually large, resources combined with the possibility of a dedicated individual replacing many of the resources (see Insight Monitoring, at the beginning of the chapter).
- The need for the recruitment of dedicated and skilled staff and providing them with adequate resources.

Some centers of excellence may be discovered by chance after the lack of success in the core product.

- That a center of excellence grows from and is nurtured by an attitude that will never accept second best. This attitude needs to percolate throughout the company.
- To achieve the center of excellence, it may sometimes be necessary to seek out excellent suppliers of small components. Naturally the suppliers need careful watching.
- The identification of criteria that a center must match is essential. These criteria vary from company to company but will certainly include accepted best practice. In Table 7.1, a number of criteria for excellence are listed in one particular product.
- All this applies to service as well as manufacturing companies.

Chapter 8. Staffing: The Innovative Atmosphere

This chapter faces four issues.

- Recruitment. Look for an unconventional character after ensuring that the company possesses an innovative atmosphere into which the recruit will fit.
- However unconventional, the recruits must *fit*—make themselves at home—among their new colleagues.
- Even so, there has to be room for friction, which a key person will keep within reasonable limits.
- Where possible, recruits should be hired on a fixed-term basis so that their ability to contribute to the company's quest for excellence can be carefully appraised before offering a permanent appointment.

Chapter 9. In-House or Contracting Out?

Is every effort made to produce the required goods and services in-house or is subcontracting usually advisable? Two opposing views are contrasted with the conclusion:

- Subcontract where possible without ignoring home-grown talent. Check whether in-house developments can be produced quickly enough.

Other principles are:

- Exploit "redundant" skill or knowledge where possible. Only subcontract where commercially essential.
- Avoid doctrinaire attachment to in-house or contracting. Profitable excellence is the only criterion. Timing is all important.
- You persuade the world to beat a path to your door by:

    —building up a reputation, a slow and painful process
    —design expertise (see Chapter 10)
    —sympathy for the customer
    —a command of ancillary products or services

A new product report at the end of the chapter shows an attempt to produce a center of excellence in a small company at three stages before the final customer.

Chapter 10. Design

This chapter confirms the widely held view that designers are the key figures in developing a center of excellence. Design suggestions must be accompanied by an affordable budget (equal to a proposal that is relative to the size of the company and the scale of the project).

Traditional designs (for example, museum properties) are rapidly being turned into saleable products.

Chapter 11. Technical Research

Technical research is another essential ingredient in a center of excellence. This chapter passes lightly over well-known problems about stimulating research and ensuring that it is constrained within the firm's objectives.

- International comparisons are mentioned as well as an excellent example of a brief commission for technical research.
- The need for crisp, direct, and meaningful briefings is addressed.
- Avoid creating a backlog in the research and development department by contracting out specialist components.
- Enthusiastic support is needed for both internal and external projects.

- Research in the service industries, especially retailing, is an important part of the national research effort. In present conditions a complacent retailer can easily go under.
- Look to research when it is obviously needed. Do not be bounced by fashion.

Chapter 12. High Tech

Electronic equipment (computer hardware), medical drugs, and equipment to improve the environment are all unveiling gaps in the marketplace if you are into these business sectors or ambitious to enter them, watch out for the gaps.

Success comes through the narrowest concentration on a section of the marketplace.

Chapter 13. New Products by Branding: Basic Industries

In basic industries, branding may replace innovation. In farming, changing crops may give a temporary boost to incomes; a wider use for the new crops is essential if the boost to prices is to offer the farmer or market gardener a viable income on a long-term basis.

Chapter 14. Services

If you are in one of the ancient professions (traditional professions such as law and accountancy), why not diversify into consultancy?

Service products cannot be stockpiled, but why not try to find a way? Experience, for instance, is a form of stockpiling but requires careful storage to make it valid.

If you are in the hospitality and tourism business, a major challenge is to update your facilities in line with modern international practice.

Chapter 15. Market Research

Market research is an essential part of new product development, but *do not* underestimate the costs.

For small companies, simple investigations can provide adequate information but the research must be reliable enough to warrant the capital investment required, including launch costs.

For developing markets, an examination of the existing supply system may be adequate.

Chapter 16. Companies and Governments

Competition legislation is universal but problems are caused by discretionary elements. Most industrialized country governments have or will have a competition law—in a system based on free competition, companies must compete freely and any attempt to restrict competition will incur legal intervention. This mostly affects large companies but small companies should be wary of falling afoul of the law.

This form of state intervention is usually noncontroversial in theory, but gives rise to controversies in practice because there are no hard and fast rules.

Chapter 17. Failure

This is a brief chapter which we hope will not affect our readers, although the consideration that we are proposing high risks is important.

Chapter 18. Investing in New Product Development

- This arises from obsolescence (planned or otherwise) anticipated when technical change compels changes in related products (saucepans, flour, typewriters, and cables are cited as examples from common experience).
- Stemming from a decision on a long-term development program, the investment decision covers both long- and short-term programs depending on the horizon of the business sector.
- The investment appraisal procedures must give a clearly positive answer for the project to go ahead.

Chapter 19. The Product Launch: Looking Ahead, Some Ethical Issues

This chapter begins with a quotation that is understood to mean that what the named company needed was a vision for the future, which gave a period of peace and quiet during which a company with enormous resources could be reoriented. Much of the chapter is devoted to the putting together of a policy for a product launch. The chapter ends with a few paragraphs on ethical issues.

PART I:
FINDING NEW PRODUCTS

The first two chapters set the scene—what do we mean by new product development and how do we make it happen? These chapters mark the horizon, as it were, for the successful developments and centers of excellence discussed in Parts II and III.

A vital, active organization can and will ensure a flow of new products, but this comes about through an innovative and pioneering spirit throughout the firm.

The finding of new products should consist of the sifting of ideas that crowd around. This, a topic of Chapter 2, is a clue to progress. Strive to maneuver yourself into a place where new products find you and not the other way around. Your role is to umpire between attractive offers.

Chapter 1

Innovation: A Relentless Thrust

A committee is a group that keeps the minutes and wastes hours.

Milton Berle

"Jones, that is a super idea." The president of a large technological corporation is speaking. "I don't know whether it should be reported at once to the chief executive or written up for the next meeting of the Product Development Committee. We must make our own products obsolete before our competitors do!" In that saying, the speaker contrasts the role of a committee with that of the chief executive.

We all have a fund of sayings and memories expressing or ridiculing committees, fueled perhaps by a guilty feeling that we would not like to have been left out of one. But our world is run by committees—what else is a cabinet, a board of directors, a football team, or a research group? No doubt a world run by committees is ten times more efficient, more worth living in, as well as less corrupt and less terrifying than a world run by dictators. We tirelessly quote such sayings as, "A camel is a horse designed by a committee." We could also say that a mouse is like a horse designed by a dictator, and we have seen companies run by dictators who have left someone else to clear up the mess they've caused. These days there is apt to be too much emphasis on personalities. We place great emphasis on personalities ourselves but we are not looking for companies managed by mice.

The point is, as we also know instinctively, a committee is a route to profitable progress but it can lead to frustration unless properly organized and managed—and that is why these words start a book on the quest for new products. The problem is to find a means of producing results from a range of bodies and to tap the wisdom and experience available to the company without causing gridlock.

A committee will not produce a successful new product; its role is to screen ideas and to assist the project leaders who are responsible for converting the ideas to profitable ends by monitoring their progress. In business a leader will usually be appointed by higher management—although, hopefully, with an eye to the need for a satisfactory rapport with the committee. Some committees are led by charismatic characters whose sheer force of personality makes them acceptable without special appointment, but most of the bodies to be considered do come together in a formal way. Who are these "charismatic" characters? Nowadays the word is used freely in the press to describe individuals who stand out to such an extent that people instinctively follow them. It was widely remarked that the deaths of Princess Diana, Mother Teresa, and Sir George Solti in the early autumn of 1997 robbed the world of three charismatic individuals in one week. The word "charismatic" was first used by a German sociologist who devised a theory of organization while at the same time practicing what he preached: he reorganized the German hospital system after Germany's defeat in 1918 in World War I.

The purpose of these introductory remarks is to emphasize that proposals for new products need project leaders who are personally answerable for the acceptance and success of their projects while the leaders, themselves, are answerable to committees or groups carefully selected from relevant experts to stimulate and control the leaders.

It is almost certain that some people will be appointed to high office while lacking "charisma" and will have to earn the right to be heard. No one can assume that he or she will automatically practice leadership in the way hoped or gain the confidence of associates without winning it. No one really knows how to turn ordinary individuals into charismatics, but later chapters will present some ideas and at least one striking example in each chapter.

Chapter 16 directly faces questions about the recruitment and training of innovators. Chapters 17 and 18 cover the insights to be derived from technical and market research—essential elements in innovation like the rest of the book.

New Product Development is made up of nineteen chapters in four parts which takes the reader through the body of knowledge and inspiration that marks the quest for new products. The rest of this part emphasizes the need for leadership and sorts out the organizational framework to make it work.

Part II brings into this framework the factors that produce success and profit including the ideas and strategies. This is followed by "centers of excellence" (Part III). What are they and what are they not? The high-sounding title covers also some more routine but no less necessary chapters on subjects such as whether to produce in-house or to contract out, and decisions on design and materials. Staffing is also considered in this part (Chapter 8) which is then followed by Part IV: along with a glimpse at "facing failures" (Chapter 17) as well as manufacture and primary industries. Part IV takes in the service sector, while chapters in this part also focus on market research, Chapter 15, relationships with governments, Chapter 16, facing failures and investment, Chapter 18, while the book ends with a forward-looking Chapter 19, "Where do we go from here?" which summarizes the whole and takes its ideas into the future.

But where do we look first for the innovation without which our company goes into slow decline? That is the main question asked in this chapter. Today's marketing success quickly becomes tomorrow's failure and that is issue one in our program. As soon as the latest marketing success has been launched, someone—*one* person—is detailed to look for a modification to take over as soon as sales show signs of flagging and to make the product obsolete before the competition do so. That person will be the focal point of a team (call it "committee" if you like) given the boundaries in product design and in dates during which a new product must be designed, produced, and launched—or the equivalent for a service industry. If the program leaves you a little breathless, so be it; it is not your lung power but the company's progress that is on the agenda. The timing must be tight to allow space for the next innovation.

Let us be clear that innovation is an executive job, and not usually a staff job. The young people in the staff planning department are there to provide facts, evidence, thought power, and general backup to the team leader. The team leader has been detailed to have the new product or service ready on time and to report (if on this issue only) directly and often to the chief executive who *will ensure that innovation is on the agenda for every board meeting.*

The innovating executive's committee will not be called a waste of time because its discussions will be efficiently prepared with a summary of proposals and a background support for each item. It will be deeply imbued with the need for a relentless thrust. There will also be timings for all the items according to their importance or immediacy. Thus a committee timed to last 100 minutes and with ten items, for example, will not allocate ten minutes to each item but a longer period for the more important ones. To illustrate, a Cambridge (England) college council [board of directors] once met to consider an agenda with two main items: (1) considering a new building and (2) appointing a new master [chief executive]. While the new building would be standing beside buildings that had already stood for over 500 years, the new master was to succeed predecessors whose average tenure had been between four and five years. The council [committee] spent four hours deciding on the new master and ten minutes considering the plans for the new building, which many of them disliked once it had been completed. This is an example of how not to manage the time of a committee. However, the college might not have survived another five years if an inadequate headmaster had been appointed.

A professional organization will normally have a partner looking out for new products while a manufacturing concern will have a marketing manager who will be offering new ideas to the most suitable among the product managers. While new product inspiration comes mainly from the marketers, it is not uncommon for suggestions to come from the shop floor via production management.

THREE LEVELS OF INNOVATIVE VISION

To maintain an effective flow of new products, those who run a business must exercise intelligent vision on three levels: the broadest long-term strategy, the strategy for product or service supremacy, and the tactics for maintaining the lead.

The broadest long-term strategy has been practiced by British Aerospace in an attempt to maintain a twenty-five-year forward view on the future of civil and military air travel, both worldwide and in outer space.

In the field of civil aviation, it is economical to transport the largest number of people or the biggest quantity of freight in one craft. How long and how far can the expansion of heavier-than-air machines be built to fly double current payloads safely and economically?

Could it be safer and more economical to move large numbers of people rocket-fashion up into space from, say, New York City, and let the spacecraft descend directly onto Tokyo? In other words, will the flight of today's jets, which is the flat trajectory of the dart, be replaced by the up-and-down trajectory of the mortar bomb in far quicker time than at present? If, in the future, fewer, more costly, larger machines are developed to move, say, 1,000 people, could this create substantial increases in demand for smaller, shorter-haul aircraft to handle journeys between London and Amsterdam?

If the broadest long-term strategy worked out by British Aerospace, Dassault, Boeing, McDonnell Douglas, and Lockheed is faulty, billions of pounds and dollars will get locked up in plants and tooling which will become prematurely derelict.

Hindsight is easy. Could better vision of the broadest long-term strategy have avoided the mass of derelict coal mines across many countries? Perhaps the captains of the American and the British coal industries should have spent more time bringing down the costs of coal-derived products such as carbon fibers, synthetic rubber, and motor car fuel. Similarly, could the hundreds of discarded steel works all over the world have been avoided if the trend toward plastics and the demand for high performance metals had been foreseen a decade or two before it happened?

Chairpersons can cultivate and improve their vision of the broadest long-term strategy by investing in pure research within the field of the industry and possibly investing in other businesses that show evidence of pioneering techniques likely to come to fruition in twenty years' time.

PRODUCT AND SERVICE SUPERIORITY

In the food and drink industry, where most innovation is a variety of existing products, the tactic is to create a stream of new products to increase profitable market share. For example, the Mars Confectionery Group, traditionally renowned for chocolate bar products, have moved into the boxed chocolates sector of the market by launching a new brand called Celebrations. The Celebrations box contains miniature world famous bar products such as Mars Bar, Milky Way, and others, all in their traditional wrappings. Meantime one of their formidable competitors, Cadbury Schweppes, is widening its range of bar products by launching Shush, containing a lightly whipped nougatine smothered in milk chocolate.

In the consumer durables field, one of the largest cutlery manufacturers in the world, Richardson of Sheffield, now part of the Macpherson Group of Australia, specializing in kitchen knives, has a product supremacy strategy which is implemented by striving to develop enough new products annually to increase profitable sales volume by 15 percent. This requires innovation in several product areas which include quality standards and price levels, edge geometry, design, edge durability, and professional and domestic uses.

The tactics for maintaining the lead are handled skilfully by Tesco stores in the United Kingdom. The first shop was opened by the founder, Jack Cohen, in 1919. At the age of twenty-one, with only £30 ($45), he was demobilized after service with the Royal Air Force in World War I. His tactics were "Stack it high and sell it cheap." Today, the Tesco Group operates over 600 stores and serves 50 million customers. Goods are no longer sold cheap but at attractive prices that make the product a good value for the money.

Tesco's own branded products, some subbranded "value," are on sale alongside world famous names in all product groups. Each store is moving steadily toward complete one-stop shopping. The comprehensive range of food and drink products are complemented by newspapers and magazines, toiletries and medicines, clothing and household goods, stationery and toys. Customer amenities and services feature a new attraction every month. They comprise generous car parking, a restaurant, rest rooms, a mail-box, cash machines, cashback facilities with debit cards at automatic tellers, financial services, insurance, home delivery, and gasoline at competitive prices as one goes out. In some stores, toiletries and medicines have been complemented by a full pharmacy service. Some of their stores stay open twenty-four hours a day from Monday morning until Saturday evening. Recently they have begun to display competitors' retail prices on their own price tickets to demonstrate their own cheaper offers.

All these improvements to Tesco customer service are achieved by taking the initiative to keep their "product" ahead. This is not done by copying competitors, but by clear forward thinking and a continuous thirst for doing or making things better.

The same stay-ahead tactics can be seen in the development of the simple hammer. Originally, since ancient times, a wooden shaft has been slotted into a metal head. The leading manufacturers can now produce a steel shaft fused into the head so securely that it will take the weight of a suspended truck without coming apart. Other improvements include a rubber handle to absorb shock for the comfort of the striker and a specially tempered face to prevent metal splinters from shooting from the head at sonic speeds.

In reviewing the three levels of innovative vision, we have mentioned several business operations in manufacture, extraction, and services. None of these enterprises are unique. Similar businesses abound in the United States and other industrialized countries. They are quoted as passing examples.

The points we make are: first, if you don't watch the far future, you could be creating disasters for your successors. Second, you must keep up a flow of new products to hold and increase your profitable market share. Third, for a product or service to win constantly, ways and means of improving it have to be brainstormed out and then made to happen before competitors can move.

In completing this opening and leading into the next chapter let us look at how and where innovations come to be noticed.

Service Industries

In retailing, innovations are found in a new product mix or layout of premises and in customer value and customer amenities.

In professional organizations the range of services is extended away from the traditional; thus medical practices are now adding nursing services, physiotherapy, and counseling. The stimulus in this case has come from changes in the law, enabling entrepreneurial doctors to provide these services. In the case of accountants, legislation has in some countries made it difficult to launch new activities; even so, some may undertake financial advice to add to their traditional auditing and tax services. In fact, most large accounting practices possess a wholly owned business consulting firm.

Among other services, transport is a special case. Trains and planes already offer a choice of basic and premium (first-class) facilities. Passenger shipping lines have had to reduce their products to ferries or tourism cruises as a result of competition from the airlines.

Surely other options could be offered that would use existing resources profitably. One attempt that has not yet established itself (its ability to provide the alternative service) is to turn a ship into a prison, even though the ship must surely be proof against escapes for all but the most expert swimmers. In *Great Expectations,* Dickens mentions the "prison hulk" lying offshore. This shows how scarce really new ideas can turn out to be.

There has hardly been a new invention in the confectionery industry since the Mars Bar of the 1930s. Most so-called new confectionery products are variations of old recipes.

A manufacturing firm is looking for actual products which appear new to the customers. In these days, burgeoning public relations (itself a significant service industry) can give new images to old objects to give them a new lease on life.

Extractive Industries: Oil, Coal, Minerals, and Agriculture

The coal industry has always been diversified into different types of coal suiting different customers—either hard coal (or anthracite) for factories, steam engines, and other uses in furnaces with heavy blasts to acquire maximum heat with maximum economy *or* soft coal for domestic grates. When it became clear that both these traditional uses were disappearing, efforts were made to diversify into treated coals such as briquettes which could be used in domestic grates and would be legal in smokeless zones.

Agriculture is an interesting, indeed dramatic, example of an industry changing its products partly to keep up with changing customer tastes but also, in Europe, in response to legislation designed to reduce farm subsidies. Diversification is being strongly recommended to farmers. Some of this will come through genetically modified foods which remain controversial in some countries.

The issues for the basic industry are examined in more detail in Chapter 13 and the scene is now set for Chapter 2—"Making Innovations Happen." The details of the process, the recruitment and training of innovators, are to be unearthed later. Here, in these early chapters, we look at the final aim of the dynamic, thrusting organization. We all take that view of our organization but a short visit by an expert consultant will reveal a different scene. A general atmosphere in which no one is hopeful, but everyone remembers the efforts that have been tried and achieved nothing will soon say: here is a no hope company requiring drastic treatment, a root and branch restart. But even someone who is not a consultant can deduce this from the operating figures. A management that cannot point to added value is doomed.

This book looks at new product development in the light of a simple body of knowledge. The whole body with chapter references is set out in Figure 1.1.

Innovation—The Road to Expansion

This chapter is mainly designed as a scene setter. What is the body of knowledge that should be absorbed by the expert on new product development?

To round off this chapter, here is an innovation review provided by a company that has been keeping innovation on its agenda.

THE BOWERS GROUP: A SUBSIDIARY OF SPEAR AND JACKSON PLC.

The Bowers Group Plc., based in Bradford, England, is a specialist in metrology, the science and systems of weights and measures. The group manufactures and markets a wide range of instruments designed to measure components of machines, vehicles, aircraft, spacecraft, fasteners, and a whole variety of scientific, electronic, and mechanical paraphernalia sometimes to the accuracy of a thousandth of a millimeter. Their history of steady expansion in the face of formidable competition has involved development from an early speciality in bore gauges used for measuring the inside diameter of holes to a wide variety of instruments for use wherever extreme accuracy of measurement is imperative. The basic product range now includes internal micrometers, cylinder bore gauges, depth gauges, hardness testers, level testers, instruments to measure screw threads, splines, and grooves, external and internal callipers, and instruments used for setting machines accurately before use.

The company was established over half a century ago and was family-owned until acquired by Spear and Jackson Plc. in 1999. It

[Chapter 1]
What it's all about

BASIC
ISSUES

[Chapter 2]
A personal drive to make innovations happen

[Chapter 3]
Success; what is required in more detail

[Chapter 4]
Timing: the roots for new products

PROCESS

[Chapter 5]
Ideas: the roots for new products

[Chapter 6]
Product development is part of corporate strategy

[Chapter 7]
Centers of excellence, a major development

EXCELLENCE

[Chapter 8]
The recruitment and training of innovators

[Chapter 9]
In-house or contracting out, a crucial decision

[Chapter 10]
Designs, one of the essentials

ISSUES

[Chapter 11]
Research, another of the essentials

[Chapter 12]
Innovations in high-tech industry

[Chapter 13]
Basic industries have basic problems

INDUSTRY
SECTORS

[Chapter 14]
The special situation of the service industries

[Chapter 15]
Market research for all industry sectors

[Chapter 16]
Relations between governments and companies

OTHER
ISSUES
AND

[Chapter 17]
Failure and how to cure it

[Chapter 18]
Investing in new product development

CONCLUSION

[Chapter 19]
Conclusion and summary; the end of the process
in the product launch; also some ethical questions
along the way

FIGURE 1.1. Unraveling the Body of Knowledge: The Framework for Understanding Innovation

employs 110 people and has a sales turnover of £8m ($12m). Spear and Jackson is a group which has acquired most of the renowned United Kingdom manufacturers of hand tools, mechanics tools, gauges, hacksaw blades, machine knives, and agricultural implement blades. It is a division of U.S. Industries Incorporated.

Bowers operates in a highly competitive price-sensitive market, dominated by the giant Mitutoyo of Japan and Tesa of Switzerland. Its progress is assumed to be due to the relentless thrust of product innovation.

A strong card in the Bowers' pack is its long-standing partnership with Sylvac of Switzerland which specializes in electronically operated metrology equipment with built-in digital displays capable of showing and recording readings with minute accuracy. The backbone of Bowers' strategy in recent years has been to exploit the combination of its own skills in metrology with the electronic expertise of Sylvac.

Such an arrangement as the partnership of Bowers and Sylvac requires cooperation and forethought. Total reliance on Sylvac could leave Bowers bereft of an electronics supplier, should the partnership break down for any reason. While if Bowers overly developed a second source, Sylvac could move toward supplying the competition. Every possible effort is made to maintain a partnership beneficial to both companies.

Perseverance with the strategy of continuous innovation led to the 1998 launch of Bowers' System Synergy, a new family of thirteen products aimed at providing their customers with a complete range of electronically driven gauges and other measuring instruments capable of not only visual display but recorded printout also.

The range is a mixture of new products together with some traditional items which were redesigned to contain the major performance benefits of the new lines, and to reflect the System Synergy family appearance. According to the catalogue, System Synergy products include a micrometer, electronic callipers, digital gauges and indicators, all of these measure to accuracies of a tenth to a hundredth of a millimeter and some to a thousandth.

System Synergy was designed to provide the customers with all their metrology needs in one delivery from under one roof. It also strengthened the company's ability to compete with Mitutoyo who, through combining manufacture with merchanting, offer a vast range of instruments. An important feature of the launch of System Synergy is a twenty-five-minute video presentation of the products in action and a catalog which enables the customer to equate the measuring task to the choice of instrument.

Bowers has maintained a steady flow of new products since the launch of System Synergy. These include the Bowers Digi-Thread, an instrument which will measure both the thread diameter of a screw together with the depth of the thread in one operation. This product is equipped with an electronic digital read out.

The Bowers Group approach to innovation has always been simple and direct. Good suggestions, mainly for product improvement, come from the production area. Most ideas, however, originate from people closest to the market or as the result of generous expenditure on technical and market research conducted both in-house and by outside specialists.

In the days of family ownership, all ideas were submitted directly to the chairman. In conjunction with other directors he carried out preliminary assessments to be sure they were worthy of further investigation and planning. If they were, the ideas would be developed into project proposals complete with budget, and placed before the product development committee.

The product development committee still exists today and is convened every two weeks. Its role is first to screen project proposals in detail, ensuring that they are compatible with Bowers as well as Spear and Jackson group strategy. The role is also responsible for monitoring the progress of each project through to launch date.

Recently, compatibility with Spear and Jackson group strategy has created a new initiative for Bowers with potential for far-reaching profitable expansion. This is already proving fruitful with the establishment of Bowers Metrology Systems.

Bowers Metrology Systems is a separate business center set up alongside the original company in Bradford. Its mission is to provide all Bowers metrology functions as instrumentation fully integrated into the production flow lines and processes of its manufacturer customers. This enables all the vital measurement checks to be carried out automatically and continuously throughout the manufacturing cycle, rather than maintaining control of quality by means of hand-held gauges.

Benefits to the customer include: First quality assurance can be checked whenever necessary without increasing the manpower in the quality assurance area. Flaws can then be detected in the product at the earliest stage of faulty processing. This enables relevant defects in the plant to be pinpointed and corrected before they cause serious damage and wasteful down-time.

Bowers Metrology Systems is marketing and selling its technical skill directly into both existing and new plants. After carrying out an installation it is more than probable that Bowers will be asked to undertake maintenance and to provide replacement instrumentation when necessary. Moreover, the customer is likely to turn to the company for such hand-held gauges as are still required.

Bowers Group salespeople seek out prospects for Bowers Metrology Systems. When customer interest is established, a highly qualified sales engineer follows up to plan and negotiate installation.

Eventually Bowers Metrology Systems could become the larger part of the Bowers business. The integration of metrology instrumentation in production processes is an established practice in the United States and Japan. The rest of the world is there for Bowers to sell into.

Bowers has a research and development department which is equipped with computer-aided design facilities. It is staffed by three research and development engineers and a very experienced manager, who reports to the production director. Most of their work is in the field of new products but they are expected to support any activity requiring technical expertise whether as part of progress or dealing with problems. In addition to computer-aided design equipment the team has an appropriate plant for the creation of prototypes. Continuous and active contribution toward innovation, however, is a way of life for all Bowers' employees.

While it features a multitude of measuring capabilities, Bowers' center of excellence is still in its roots: the perfection of hand-held and plant-integrated gauges performing to minute degrees of accuracy. This excellence has pervaded into every product in the Bowers' range—accuracy to exceptional tolerances with consequent quality supremacy.

There is an acute awareness of the need to keep up with the ever-changing demands created by the technical innovation of customer industries and to satisfy these before competitors do so.

But for the continuous quest for expansion into new products, the Bowers Group might have had to survive by lowering its quality standard in order to sell on price. Such survival would probably be only temporary as a policy of selling on price could have led to the company being ploughed under by its larger competitors. The company with the support of Spear and Jackson Plc. is now in a solid niche of a vast market, a niche not for sheltering but one in which there is ever-changing scope for further profitable expansion such as production line integrated instrumentation as marketed by Bowers Metrology Systems.

This review of the Bowers operation raises points for the reader's consideration:

- Are we under pressure from competition on price? If so, are we being sucked into the "rat race," or are we able to stay in front by restricting our market to a niche in which we can sell high quality for a profitable price?
- Have we invested sufficiently in computer-aided design equipment and plant for producing prototypes in our research and development department?
- Can we sell the excellence of our product or service into our customer's businesses and make income from training their employees to use it?
- Can we honestly claim that innovation is a way of life among all our employees?

Chapter 2

Making Innovations Happen

It is always the latest song that an audience applauds the most.

Homer

   The *project group* is a very specialized kind of committee because it has been formed for a limited purpose; its members are those considered most able to promote this purpose. Its leader is normally a product or brand manager, who has already established his or her authority by the handling of existing products. To the product manager's existing duties is added the finding of a new product and this will be done in the realization that the manager's career is at stake. A new and saleable product plan complete with specifications, costs, promotional requirements, and timings is the main job and priority of the team leader (product manager).

   Have no doubt that the thrust and drive of the project group is the key to making innovations happen. No unnecessary restrictions must be placed on the group in order to avoid reducing its dynamism, except that strict limits must be placed on the duration of meetings. Expensive executives cannot be kept sitting around while all the members insist on having their say. A system needs to be in place within which the new product leaders, groups, and committees can be developed and can work efficiently—without unnecessary let or hindrance. The establishment of such a system is an important theme of this book and those who are in a position to place "lets or hindrances" need to be restrained from doing so. New product innovation is a basic requirement of any corporate strategy.

   Yesterday "product managers" were lesser gods looking after particular brands or "products" for their companies. In many service industries, such as lawyers and accountants, the equivalent officers do not have special titles but are regarded as partners with special responsibilities. Recently both authors received a glimpse of the future when they encountered product managers who were regarded as close to board level, advising the chief executive on major new developments vitally affecting the future of their companies.

The emergence of the new style product manager, handling moves into new products, is ensuring that product development is taking a more dynamic place in the corporate order. The recruiting, training, and organizing of the innovators is explained in Chapter 8, but here we concern ourselves with the thrusting leadership sitting on top of this "dynamic place." The members of the team will all be busy executives who have built up reputations in their existing jobs. Each will have a specific responsibility in the project team related to their appointment in the company. In the case of a manufacturing company, there will be specialists in either the manufacturing process or the product. Marketing will also be represented. The difference between a project group and any other committee is this element of appointment and representation; members will have a definite time allocated to the new product activity and papers will be prepared for each meeting.

Let us sit in on a typical meeting.

AN EXAMPLE: TERROFIN INC.

Terrofin Inc. (fictitious name) specializes in making chemical substances for finishing metal surfaces. The company has invented a lacquer which will permanently protect the shine on silver or silver plating. The company has decided to market this product to householders. This is its first venture outside industrial markets and into consumer markets. The product name is to be Permatone.

The project group includes the following people: Chairman, John Slack (Product Manager, Precious Metal Finishes); Production Member, Phil Piper (Assistant Production Controller); Marketing Member, Gillian Dexter (Assistant Customer Services Manager); Finance Member, Shaun Villiers (Supervisor, Accounts Payable).

All names are fictitious and were invented for the sake of this example of a company which is itself fictitious but based on numerous existing firms.

Except for the chairman, all are young, promising, management people selected for membership as part of their professional development as well as their qualifications for producing a satisfactory result.

CHAIRMAN: We have exactly four months before the launch date of Permatone. Let's look at progress. Phil, you lead, please.

PRODUCTION MEMBER: Evenness of application is still a problem. R and D [research and development] is currently working with several thinning agents to overcome this problem. Meanwhile they have come up with this dipping kit. It consists of a dish capable of holding the average item of table cutlery and forceps to grip each item while only touching it at two points with pinhead size contact. This is going to add 75p ($1.13) to the cost.

CHAIRMAN: Can you find any other savings in production to offset this cost?

PRODUCTION MEMBER: Not yet, but we are working at it.

MARKETING MEMBER: But marketing can. We are able to reduce the marketing costs if our revised plan is accepted. This is our first venture into consumer marketing and, as you know, we had envisaged a budget of $300,000 for advertising, $150,000 a year for the cost of four salesmen, and $200,000 for various launch and other expenses.

We are now devising a plan to launch and sell this product by setting up a small number of stores within stores at the leading departmental shops in London, New York, and Washington. We'll introduce the product by live demonstration. The costs of this method are far lower than advertising or the monitoring of reps [representatives] on the road. A detailed marketing plan will be available next week and we anticipate a reduction of $120,000 in marketing costs in the first year.

CHAIRMAN: Any comment, Shaun?

FINANCE MEMBER: I've seen their preliminary figures and I would have hoped for even greater savings.

MARKETING MEMBER: If you want greater savings, let's make the product more attractive. Could we have a spray applicator for silver holloware as well as the dipping dish?

CHAIRMAN: Phil? How about it?

PRODUCTION MEMBER: We began with a spray applicator, which we found unsuitable for cutlery. We worried about putting harmful chemicals into the hands of people who might misuse them. But we could make it for about $3.50; it possibly would have to be sold as an optional extra.

MARKETING MEMBER: We are too far advanced with the packaging of the product and dipping kit to alter it. I agree, the spray applicator would be a very attractive optional extra, especially for store demonstration. This would increase sales revenue without incurring additional marketing costs.

FINANCE MEMBER: I know its not my affair, John, but listening to Phil and Gillian, I believe you should get the board to maintain the original high budget despite proposed savings. You must allow for slippage.

CHAIRMAN: OK, I agree. Now what about timing?

MARKETING MEMBER: We really must keep to a pre-Easter launch, to get the full impact of in-store demonstrations.

CHAIRMAN: Before we close, let's go through the CPA [Critical Path Analysis] to check through every detail and timing point.

In this story the following six stages are assumed.

Stage 1. An idea is passed to the product development committee or directly to the board.

Stage 2. The idea is accepted and a budget and a tentative timetable is proposed.

Stage 3. The board appoints a project group to make it happen.

Stage 4. Work of the project group is carried out, with frequent progress checks by the product development committee.

Stage 5. Consumer or user trials before launch.

Stage 6. Launch.

Each stage implies a dynamic driving force somewhere to make it happen. Without this the project will be lost in a filing cabinet (or a hard disk).

The story is also a snapshot of a continuing process, a process that always interests top management because the future of the company under its present management depends on a successful resolution. Lose out on the new product development and the share price will slide, laying the firm open to takeover. A rights issue, if needed, will then become more expensive and existing shareholders will become discontented.

Chapter 5 will explore the origin of ideas that stimulate the project at the outset.

One item should not be forgotten—timing. There is the personal timing for the people involved as well as the timing for the market. If the chairman was about to retire, he or she might not be so willing to take the long-term view. He or she may have reached a stage when strong pressure from colleagues is required for the necessary longer-term view.

The product timing requires that a number of questions about the product be answered, including:

1. Is there a worthwhile market for this product, and are we targeting a substantial share of it?
2. Will this product have market acceptance? How unusual is it? Or is it a new version of an old product?
3. Have we found a launch date that will give the new product the best chance of success, and can we meet it?
4. Is it known that the product is a winner but that we are running up to launch neck and neck with a dangerous competitor? If so, how can we get in first if we need to? One particular danger is that a competitor getting in first may steal our reputation.
5. What else is known about the competition that would affect our timing?
6. Have the costs of marketing been realistically calculated? It would be easy, for instance, to underestimate the cost of an in-store shop.
7. Have we allowed time for the marketing program and made the necessary arrangements for it through user or consumer trials?

These questions arise in connection with a manufacturing product, but similar questions apply to service industries, especially those that are linked to the readiness of the market and the state of the competition; with some service industries (a professional body or a retailer) the question of timing is more difficult and more critical. In the case of a professional organization, the budget is unlikely to be large enough to control sufficiently the timing of the launch.

The critical element in the story is the appointment of product managers (by whatever name they are called) who have demonstrated the breadth of vision and the commitment to mastermind the whole development with the knowledge that their future depends upon the performance of the product.

GENEVAC LIMITED

The creation of the Genevac Company and its outstanding success are the result of the determination of an experienced inventor, capably supported by his family to eliminate the bottlenecks in the evaporation process in busy drug laboratories.

To appreciate the significance of this achievement one has to be aware of the intensity of the search for new drugs all over the world.

Much of this activity is carried out by large, wealthy pharmaceutical companies, who have the resources to organize research on a massive scale, involving thousands of experimental samples per day.

Doctor Michael Cole, a physicist, who founded Genevac Limited, has been an inventor all his working life. Aided by his wife, Susan, who has provided his administrative backup, he formed or acquired one company after another to develop and market his inventions. Not all his efforts have been crowned with success; he has experienced the trauma of selling house and property to clear business debts. His grit and ability to bounce back has led to the success of Genevac today and the benefit it has created for the pharmaceutical industry.

The founder also invented the Cole pump involving a new pumping principle which is described later together with Genevac's products. As a laboratory pump, it has played an important part in Genevac's current operation. The company, however, became sidetracked into developing a much larger version than the original laboratory pump because of strong interest shown by oil companies.

Because the Cole pump is the only pump with one moving part that can pump both liquid oil and gas, company executives could see a developed version being used for pumping mixtures of oil and gas direct from the sea bottom to settling tanks on shore. At present, tanks the size of a football field have to be built in deep water over the wells to separate the gas and oil so that conventional pumps can pump them ashore. These oil rigs cost $1 billion at currently exploited depths and much more at greater depths. Such a pump would be able to open up deeper fields and shallower small fields where in both cases the current cost of rigs makes them uneconomic.

The apparent good luck of the successful development of the pumps was followed by a change in policy on the part of the board of a major oil company, illustrating a problem of a small company selling to a large company, when the development was suspended in favor of concentration on short-term profitability. This abrupt termination dealt a severe financial blow to the inventor, but the pump itself has played an important part in the success of Genevac's current operation.

For many years Doctor Cole had been aware of the growing problems of rapid evaporation in the "drug discovery," the term by which drug research is known in the pharmaceutical industry.

The task is to evaporate liquids from solutions, at speeds demanded by the pace or urgency of the research project, without harming the residual solids in any way.

The liquids concerned are water, various acids, and organic solvents such as alcohol. The heat caused by boiling off the liquids would be directly destructive to the solids. Removing the liquids by a static vacuum process would take off some of the solid matter with them.

Evaporation, therefore, is carried out by spinning the containers, either a form of test tube or a microtitre plate at high speed creating a steady reduction of the liquid content. A microtiter is a minute sample. A microtiter plate is a flat rectangular block of plastic into which approximately 100 cavities are bored to provide vessels for these tiny samples.

Doctor Cole's challenge was to devise a method of carefully balancing the use of spinning, vacuum, and gentle heat to achieve the best way of handling large quantities of wet samples.

As a result of his efforts, Genevac has developed a line of centrifugal evaporators, the largest of which has increased productivity in the evaporative operation one hundredfold—ten times the normal load of samples at ten times the normal speed of spinning.

Genevac Limited was established in 1990 to specialize in the manufacture of centrifugal evaporators for laboratory use in the pharmaceutical industry. The business employs seventy people and is located at Ipswich in Southeast England.

From its beginning the firm has maintained a continuous program of product development to adapt its products to the changing demands of the user market.

A company strategy is to provide innovative products to satisfy the most challenging requirements in the market through concentration on in-house research and development. In the pharmaceutical research market, the requirements are for high throughput, low maintenance, corrosion proof, flexible systems which protect the integrity of valuable samples during operation.

Through sticking to the principle of making exactly what the customer needs, the company has achieved rapid growth. Through 1998 and 2000 sales have increased by 272 percent. The export proportion of those sales increased by 290 percent. The company was awarded the Queen's Award for Enterprise in Innovation in March 2000.

The firm now makes a line of seven high performance solvent evaporation systems to satisfy the varying demands of pharmaceutical research worldwide.

The first the DD4 Centrifugal Solvent Evaporation System is a general purpose machine for use in research laboratories. It incorporates some of the high performance features and benefits of the company's higher specification HT Series of evaporators described below. It is able to accommodate most test-tube sizes up to 150 mm and a swing rotor is available for the use of microtitre plates. The rate of evaporation is controlled by the variance of the speed of spinning and the application of controllable infrared heat. The machine has the Genevac "Aquaspeed" system to handle water and some water mixtures for which the evaporation rate can be accelerated.

The HT4 Series of Evaporator is for medicinal chemistry and drug discovery systems. These machines are designed to handle larger quantities of samples more rapidly by applying high vacuum as well as spinning and infrared heat. They automatically eliminate any imbalance resulting from the positioning of various weights of samples on the rotor. As an optional extra they can include the company's "Dri-pure" system for preventing samples spilling out of their containers. This is known as "bumping"—spillage either from one container into another causing contamination or away from the rotor area, which is wasteful. The machines are equipped with the Cole principle pump to remove the liquid drawn off the solids by the evaporation process.

The more recently designed Series HT8 and HT12 are machines designed to provide a solution for evaporative bottlenecks in busy drug discovery laboratories. Because they are equipped with multilayer rotors, they can take larger quantities of samples while provid-ing economy in laboratory bench space. The system for preventing samples "bumping" is incorporated as well as the Cole pump. The latest and largest machines are the Mega 980 and 1200 series which provide ultrahigh throughput solvent evaporation systems. They can accommodate samples in an extensive variety of microtiter plates or even smaller containers but also formats larger than a normal plate as well as a wide range of sizes of test-tubes. They are equipped with the antibumping system and the high imbalance protection. They are computer controlled and can therefore be operated on a virtually continuous basis. These machines sell in the region of £200,000 ($300,000) each, and the remaining items vary in price down to £20,000 ($30,000) for the DD4.

All the larger machines are equipped with the Cole pump which separates gases from liquids drawn off in the evaporation process. This is based on the same principle developed by Dr. Cole for under-sea oil extraction. The Cole pumping principle uses a high velocity stream of fluid in a rotating drum passing over a stationary wing-shaped foil to create a vacuum cavity at the top of the leading edge. A slot at this point on the foil allows a stream of gas or vapor to be drawn into the fluid in the form of bubbles which spiral into the cen-tral exhaust zone under centripetal force. From this atmospheric pres-sure zone the vapors have a clear passage to the exhaust of the pump.

Genevac has matched the dynamism of its product development with a global marketing and selling thrust. The dynamism of the founder-inventor has been made possible by the support of other members of his family.

In terms of marketing, the company displays its products the world over, at many exhibitions and trade fairs featuring their areas of interest: combinational and medicinal chemistry, high throughput screening, automation, synthetics, drug development and recently, genomics. The shows enable the company to demonstrate its products to a large number of potential customers. In addition, Genevac provides full in-formation on its recently upgraded Web site. The use of a feedback form for obtaining product information also facilitates the monitor-ing of the growth potential of new markets.

Direct sales are made from Ipswich to customers in Britain, the Netherlands, Belgium, France, Switzerland, and Germany. An office in Paris provides support for the French, Swiss, and Benelux markets, while an office in Frankfurt takes care of sales in Germany. The United States market, which accounts for 55 percent of total sales, is the largest market in the world for laboratory equipment designed for pharmaceutical research and development.

To keep a grip on the United States market, the company has set up a subsidiary company located near New York supported by one-person satellite offices in Boston, San Diego, San Francisco, and Louisville. Throughout the remaining markets sales are achieved through hand-picked distributors. The company foresees that, in future years, the volume of sales may create the need for Genevac subsidiaries in many of the markets handled by distributors today.

However skillful is the marketing and selling, customer cooperation is essential. The company concentrates also on providing an excellent standard of support to customers. This includes collaborative projects together with research and development activity.

The degree of success enjoyed by Genevac needs the service of very capable people. The company, therefore, has an open training strategy which provides access to further personal development to any employee who seeks it. This includes language training to strengthen sales ability in other countries.

In recent years the success of the company caused Dr. Cole to find two international corporations competing with each other to acquire the business. Eventually the equity was sold to the Sybron Corporation of the United States, which appointed Dr. Cole's son to be chief executive on his father's retirement.

Since his retirement Dr. Cole has been working on two new inventions which one day could have a beneficial impact on the food and drink industry.

This review leads to a number of questions, for instance:

1. What about our company's innovation track record?
2. Are we inventive enough and, if not, where do we get the talent?
3. Does our marketing and selling effort match our inventiveness?
4. Are we giving our employees the training needed for our projected performance for the future?

What Have We Learned from This Chapter?

People make innovations happen through their training and their personalities, and this means hard work in recruiting and training.

There is no mechanical process whereby one innovation leads to another without human intervention. Nevertheless, the company needs to establish a system that stimulates and does not frustrate the efforts of the innovators within it. The system needs to ensure that individual participants see their future to be in new product development. Business reputations have so often been made in recent years in retrenchment. This breeds an attitude that is hostile to innovation.

PART II:
MOVING ON—
SUCCESSFUL DEVELOPMENTS

"We have set up our unit in Massachusetts as a 'Center of Excellence.' " That expression has become one of the shibboleths of our times similar to "corporate strategy," "management by objectives" and many other expressions that give speakers (as well as their boards) a warm feeling that something has been achieved. And so it probably has, but the achievement is harder than the glib use of the words usually suggests.

Part II is based on the authors' observations of what can happen to new product development in firms that take it seriously. Two themes stand out: the need for speed and the need for ideas. Speed will be futile if not based on ideas. Ideas will be wasted if the timing is wrong. As the search for new products gathers momentum, the ideas will be expected to bubble up, but this will not happen automatically. While some developments may come from chance; normally human aid will be needed to reinforce the chance and make sure it turns up the right message.

At the end of Part II, Chapter 6 makes way for Part III, which is devoted to centers of excellence, the crucial part of this book.

Chapter 3

Success

Looking for success?

Of course. This chapter lists the factors that contribute to success including the famous mantra: avoid backing a declining industry. In the Executive Summary is a checklist of the items detailed—an agenda for a planning project meeting. See pages xvii through xix. The headings here correspond to those in that checklist.

SUCCESS FACTORS

Avoid Backing a Shrinking Industry

Support only growing industries. That means avoiding tobacco, trains, corsets, and cinemas, does it? One obvious success factor, you may say, is not to diversify into unwanted products. But wait awhile and take another look at that list.

Tobacco

There are huge populations that have not yet reached sufficient wealth to become customers of the tobacco companies who continue to make profits out of a product now discredited in the rich countries. They are constantly opening fresh markets before they diversify further. Immoral, did I hear you say? The ethics chapter comes later (Chapter 19), but that is not all that can be said. Research has continued to diversify into a safer product. This started with Du Maurier, brand name for the first filter-tipped cigarette. Since then, the industry has pursued in-depth research into filtration and other techniques to take out the harmful substances, the nicotine and the tar, without losing the narcotic value that is the main attraction of the product.

Trains

The notorious British train manager Lord Beeching declared that the future of the railways lay in commuters, long-distance business travel, and freight. Trains were certainly not, the puritanical lord declared (appointed by a minister who was a member of a road-building family), part of the tourist industry. His one much publicized innovation was the so-called "container train." Since then container trains have threatened losses while tourism has brought profits. The loss of employment in the motor industry is being replaced by increasing employment in the rail industry (especially equipment manufacturers). This is recorded in most industrial and industrializing countries. No less than two Japanese train builders, who also make cars, announced in 2001 that they were setting up subsidiaries to build trains in Britain.

Corsets

Corsets are an odd addition to this list, you might well think. However, Spirella, the main corset company in Britain, employed over 25,000 part-time women to fit the product to the customer. The company then diversified into related products that used the same skills, such as swimsuits. It may be obsolete now but the simple corset carried a course on marketing within itself. A clothing company may well find a niche in the market which involves some garment purpose fitted at the customer's home. As long as people exist, there is likely to be a market for foundation garments. These will change, as they have in the past, by changes in fashion for figures, including the flat figure and the hourglass figure.

Cinemas

The demise of cinema was confidently predicted once micro-electronics had brought television into the reach of all, which is currently enjoying a revival. This has resulted from a skillful product policy that caters to present-day younger audiences anxious to avoid their parents' choice of television programs. Some developments in the cinema industry have hinted at further innovation. For example, three- dimensional projection has a long way to go before it is perfected. Another example is the attachment of smell to a film to make, for instance, the fresh smell of the countryside or the foul smell of the battlefield add realism to the visual and verbal aspects of the film which then stimulates three senses (sight, hearing, and smell).

Life Cycles: Watching the Life Cycles of Existing Products and Projects

Some authorities regard this as the most significant success factor. The job of product managers is to be ever-vigilant on the life cycle watch, noting the gradual decline of volume or profitability of a product after it encounters more competition. Product managers need to be trained to make a high commitment to their products but must also possess an ability to propose a new product even before the danger signs appear, signs which they should be the first to see. One sign is a decline of revenue from a product even while sales continue to increase; another is the need to cut prices to maintain worthwhile volume. Service industries will naturally also be vigilant in watching for opportunities for diversification. Credit cards are an example of sustained efforts to remain in the market with comparatively minor adjustments to the product to expand the market. These adjustments include changing designs in order to make the cards collectors' pieces as British Telecom have achieved with their phone cards. Other minor adjustments include changing interest rates (not of great concern to those who repay regularly) and the dates from which interest is charged.

The Opportunity for Meeting an Unsatisfied Demand

Is this the positive side of life cycle vigilance? At some time in our industrial history some genius noticed an unsatisfied demand for liquid soap. Once discovered, this product gradually diversified into shower gel and hand-washing soap, for instance.

Matches Contemporary Market Scene

Even if it is not possible to foresee the future, timing can make the difference between success and failure as it has for the Italian-designed new style tramcars. These were an adaptation of their maker's product range at a time when this form of public transportation was beginning to be sought by transport operators desperate to overcome the gridlock in their cities and to develop a product less costly than trains and faster than buses.

Uses More Effectively a Company's Existing Resources (Staff, Cash, Reputation)

This principle is not always as simple as it looks. Say, for example, that you manage a chain of sports shops. You will find yourself embroiled in so many of the problems that point to innovation as fashions change. You will watch the Olympic Games and note that your stocks of guns are rapidly becoming obsolete, but restocking now will be subject to gun laws, whereas an inability to sell equipment for synchro-swimming—a sport rapidly becoming more popular—will drive would-be customers to other shops. Special clothing for other sports will remind you of fashion clothing for cyclists. In fact, one sports shop proprietor said, "Mine is a fashion business. I sell to affluent young trendsetters."

Carefully Thought-Out Design Picks Up on a Company's Existing Image

Sports retailers know all about company images. Clothing in their house style will be caught by television cameras and beamed into thousands of homes. Other baggage can gradually be added to the package as football clubs such as Manchester United and sports shops on both sides of the Atlantic have already done.

Marketing gimmicks are closely linked to that last item. Free gifts and other promotions can be used to distinguish and refresh a product that has already reached nearly the end of its life cycle slide. In this case, the innovation is only to be found in the marketing. It is not a new product but a substitute for a new product. A good product at launch time, in full flight, and in early decline needs skilful marketing measures. These can even bring back a flagging product. Take Bisto as an example. This once dominated the gravy market until, more recently, it was swamped by other brands. Today it is staging a come-back with its time-honored slogan "Ah Bisto" in modern packaging, featured in topical television advertisements.

Probability of Achieving a Viable Market Share

Realistic calculations are needed to ensure that sufficient market share can be acquired over the lifetime of the new project. This applies especially if export sales are needed. Much evidence has shown that success in a foreign market depends on the market share obtained there as well as success at home, while a useful yardstick for fixing targets abroad is to seek the same (or better) share in each foreign territory as at home.

Opening Up New Markets

Climate change is bringing with it unparalleled opportunities for discovering new niches. In the British climate, for instance, safeguards against the cold and the damp are always needed, but nowadays such safeguards are increasingly needed against heat and direct sunlight. The old joke about selling refrigerators to the Eskimos can be turned into selling cooling systems to the British.

A more satisfactory example is that of a shirt manufacturer, when beaten by Southeast Asian competition, the company spotted a new market in workwear for salesclerks.

Meeting an Unsatisfied Demand

Everyone's ideal new product fills a gap in the market. A supplier of personal products once noticed that the growth of alternative medicines would soon produce a fresh gap in the pharmacy market and aromatherapy oils found their way into pharmacies. This solution itself raises some questions: Does the market for this product fit our existing markets? Or: Do we have the resources (especially in sales and marketing staff) to promote it? Or again: Do we have adequate evidence of a growth in demand over the lifetime of the capital needed to support the project?

Stanley Tools in Britain was persuaded by its American parent to sell hardware such as hinges and hasps and drawer handles made by Stanley Deutschland alongside hand tools in Britain. The results were disastrous. The markets are poles apart. Bassett Foods avoided the trap of trying to sell products from its bakery subsidiaries alongside licorice allsorts.

Price: Achieving a Profitable Price

The price tag that the market will accept is compulsory (a given which you will normally have to accept); it can be manipulated as itself an innovatory signal. A key marketing principle is: The message is in the price. By this token, a product can be moved up-market by continuous stages of improvement which will give greater value and so justify price rises.

Costs

If, nevertheless, a product cannot break the chains of existing prices, a concerted attack on costs is needed to support the innovation.

Value engineering can be helpful in attacking costs. For example: "Why do we need this solid cast-iron cover, surely a plastic molding would be cheaper and lighter?" Or: "Could we not save $3.50 on each product by replacing its four bolts, four nuts, and four washers with four simple 'snap-on' joints?"

Return on Investment

Even the smallest modification can be costly. No one will wish to proceed with it unless the return on the investment placed in it is expected to exceed the average return for the company. The costs of new investment need to be assessed in total and will include the direct research and development applied to the product; that is obvious but to it must be added the cost of management time, of the interest rates on the funding, and of retraining the sales force. This is the other side to the pressure for new product development: developments must be in keeping with other objectives of the company such as return on investment. This will be calculated according to the firm's standard investment appraisal procedures.

Ability to Manage New Markets

Recent business history is full of stories of companies that have made what they considered a modest move only to find it was a much bigger step than expected—the cake maker who moved into biscuits is a case in point. Imagining that the same retail outlets would be OK for the sales force, the firm discovered that it was treading in a different world. Instead of competing with other middle-sized cake manufacturers, it was up against huge multinational biscuit manufacturers with sales forces more than a match for the representatives of less established concerns whom the retailer proved not anxious to meet. A reputation for cakes scored nothing with biscuits. Food and drinks in general are difficult markets to break into, thus making established market superiority a major success factor. Investment in new products and innovation is considered in more detail in Chapter 18.

The difficulty of breaking into new markets is a good reason for achieving innovation by acquiring a small, responsibly run company whose brands may not be the biggest sellers, but are well respected by trade and customers and sold by a competent, albeit small marketing and field sales staff.

Obsolescence

Innovation almost inevitably makes some of a company's existing products obsolete, but if nothing is made unsaleable, a firm still has to watch that a small improvement does not cost more sales in an old product than it gains for the new one. The example of electric toasters has been quoted; in attempting to develop a toaster that works more closely to the customer taste, a company can lose sales of earlier products which losses need to be costed against the success of the innovation. Under the heading of obsolescence, most firms will examine all the implications of an innovation before going ahead.

New Materials

Ability to Use New Materials

This vital factor takes into account the track record of the whole company as a constant seeker of new materials: adaptability of staff to new machinery and processing methods of a manufacturer, or of routines in the case of service industries.

Ability to Use Technical Research Costs Creatively

It is ironic that the department that is dedicated to innovation, research, and development, may be most resistant to it. This situation often arises from a personal factor: the specializations hired into the

department may be less adaptable and capable of the required breadth
of vision than is needed.

Ability to Use Market Research Effectively

A food company once planned to produce a new kind of sausage.
The team commissioned to carry out the market research, their eyes
fixed on a broader market than the sausage, came out with the proposed sales figures larger than the entire national sales for sausages.
Others have received similarly dangerous advice from market research, a subject considered more fully in Chapter 15.

Speed of Entry

A successful policy is to move into new products so relentlessly
and so quickly that neither the copier nor the patent breaker can maintain the pace. These tactics will confuse the competition.

International

A means of meeting the problems which lead to product innovation decisions is by selling abroad. This activity may require considerable adaptation to local rules and customs—so a kind of double innovation is required: adapting the product to a different market
operating in a different culture; national prejudices need to be taken
into account.

Using the Success Factors

We have set out a number of ways in which innovation can be directed to successful (more profitable) performance. Companies can
usually find a way to mobilize some of the success factors at the same
time. Their use will be more effective if combined with marketing
tactics. This applies especially to service industries.

For instance, the success of supermarkets and the surviving corner
shops, as well as the downfall of others, shows that the public sometimes reacts favorably to retail innovations. Two examples of this are:
(1) making out one's own bill on a calculator in a supermarket, and
(2) extending late-night and weekend shopping hours. The proprietor
of a Canadian corner shop told one of the authors that twenty-four-

hour opening was his main competition tactic. Innovations in retailing will usually be introduced cautiously to ensure that customers do not react unfavorably. Endless rearranging of the displays in small to middle-sized shops, designed to ensure that customers see a wider range of the merchandise available, may in fact confuse those customers and induce them to look elsewhere. Retailing that depends so much on innovation may, at the same time, take advantage of the familiar to make customers more comfortable.

All the items listed have been known to lead to successful innovation, but to do so they must be managed by an individual with the initiative and drive required to make things happen.

This chapter contains some principles that contradict other chapters, the main theme, of this book. There are salutary reminders lest we forget to take precautions and try to cut corners.

Finally, how do you know when you have a successful new product? The purpose of asking this question is to emphasize again the importance of timing. If the product is an immediate success and makes a wide impact upon the market at once, there is little need to consider whether it is a success. This will not be expected of many products. Both manufacturers and service professionals will introduce products that are not expected to make an immediate impact in their market. They will enter certain landmarks into the calendar and judge success by the speed of growth in sales of the product.

British Gas is a company that has concentrated on new product development. Its policies are outlined in the following section.

BRITISH GAS SERVICES LTD.

The British government privatized British Gas, selling it to the public as a single entity in 1986. Foreseeing the conditions likely to prevail in a competitive market, British Gas Plc. undertook in 1996 a program of reorganization to improve concentration on each of the important areas of the gas business. Again in 1996, the Gas Act demanded that the structure of distribution be separated from customer contact and that a separate division be formed. Transco was formed to specialize in exploration, production, pipelines, and distribution. In 1997 it spun off its customer service activity as an independent public company, Centrica Plc. At the time of this demerger, Centrica involved approximately a quarter of the capitalization of the group. By the year 2000, this proportion had risen to 39 percent of a rapidly expanding corporation. Within a year it acquired the Automobile Association and had created its own credit card (Goldfish) to award discounts from gas bills. In addition, by 2000 it had widened its customer service capability to handling electrical appliances, plumbing, and the installation of domestic home security systems. Centrica is now giving service to people not only in their homes but in their cars. In the words of Roger Wood (quoted from *The Economist*) the car is one of the essential services of the household. Centrica has moved from "services to the house" to "services to the household."

British Gas Services Ltd. is a subsidiary of Centrica and is the leading installer of central heating systems in the United Kingdom. Having extended its activity beyond central heating and gas appliances to kitchen appliances, plumbing, drains, and home security, it is also the leading repair and maintenance company for these services.

In 1996 the company suffered a loss of £196m ($294m). In 1997 this was reduced to £49m ($73.5m) and it earned its first-ever profit of £10m ($15m) in 1998. In 1999 this was doubled to £20m ($30m). This was achieved by a massive reduction of costs on the one hand and increase in productivity on the other.

The company moved away from twelve regional operations with their ninety districts to six operational centers handling 11 million calls per year. They are supported by a service cover membership office, a national parts center, a national central heating office and a national security office. Four hundred and forty-two depots have been closed.

Information technology has been applied to raise productivity in a business normally associated with individuals in blue overalls. Maintenance engineers no longer gather at a local depot every morning to collect spares and pick up their worksheets for the day. They now work from home and log onto a lap-top computer with a mobile phone link to take jobs as they come in to the company's call centers. The call center uses computers to help allocate work to the nearest engineer with the needed skills.

By keying the details of a faulty boiler, the engineer can read off a guide to the characteristics and parts of the particular model. This means that he has no need to carry a van full of manuals as back-up. The lap-top will signal that the replacement part has been identified and, if necessary, order it by fast post. The latest technology allows the lap-top to be plugged in to diagnose and discover the fault. Soon this will be done remotely, saving the cost of a diagnostic visit.

The lap-top will also print out the customer's bill, provide a wealth of information on more than 4,000 appliances and a multimedia magazine. The latter keeps the engineer updated with all that is going on in the company around him.

The system enables work to be transferred from an engineer who is delayed on a job to a colleague who is available to take it on. A man who was formerly carrying out four jobs per day is now averaging 7.4 jobs. Starting and finishing the day at home certainly allows more time on the job, and probably more time with the family as well.

A strong indication of improvement of customer service is that by 1998 complaints to the Gas Consumer Council had been reduced by 38 percent. Other key indicators are that all incoming calls are answered within twenty seconds; over 85 percent of all jobs are completed on the first visit; 60 percent of jobs requiring parts are completed from the engineers' van stock; and 96 percent of all work is completed within twenty-four hours. Customer satisfaction is at an all time high and still climbing. Still, the company receives complaints from dissatisfied customers but it feels able to respond more quickly, and is not complacent about this.

For its innovative thinking, the courage to undertake such sweeping changes, and the enormous investment in information technology, British Gas Services Ltd. won the Queen's Award for Enterprise in March 2000.

This achievement has not only required forward vision, sound strategic planning, exceptional skill in information technology, and bold financial risk, but also excellent leadership.

The number of employees was reduced from 25,000 to 8,000 during the five-year period of 1994 to 1999. Two hundred twenty-two different operating systems were dovetailed into a single integrated set of systems. Four hundred twenty-two reporting centers were replaced by nine offices, and eleven layers of management between engineer and managing director were reduced to six. In the area of marketing, a wide range of appliance repair products that were complicated to operate were rationalized into a smaller group of core products based around the "whole life" of central heating products. This included new installation, prompt service to fulfil service contracts, upgrade and enhancement, and replacement. This provided focus for development into new "high value" growth sectors including electrical appliances, home security, plumbing, and drains. Capacity became available for the reintroduction of on-demand servicing. The company has taken over the work of installing a variety of appliances formerly undertaken by the British Gas shops, which were closed to eliminate their losses.

One cannot achieve changes of this magnitude without the cooperation of a large number of employees. The move to core products cost 1,700 jobs. A large number of administrative posts (3,500) were no longer required and the reduction in layers of management made an additional 2,400 people redundant. These figures are only part of the massive reduction overall of 17,000 people.

Among service engineers, there was a variety of reactions to change. Some people greeted the innovation with enthusiasm; some felt they were too set in their ways to change their day-to-day routine. Some felt unable to master the lap-top, while others were eager to try but did not have the confidence their bosses had in handling computers.

After all the redundancies, early retirements, and the settling in of the lap-top scheduling system, a leadership challenge still remains. The field manager and district manager each had their teams distributed over a wide area and the teams operated fairly independently. The managers have to inculcate a team spirit and maintain enthusiasm and cooperation all round.

For the future, British Gas is doubling its intake of apprentices to two hundred a year. The company is tapping the availability of women who are single parents and can be available for service work locally while their children are at school. This development is driven by government policy and our company's involvement with the industry's national training organization.

During 2001, the patrolmen of the Automobile Association were equipped with lap-top computers to program, coordinate, and schedule their attendance to broken-down cars.

Some of our readers may take a deep look into the costs and productivity of their own businesses. They may consider following the lead of British Gas Services Ltd. and the Automobile Association. Before attempting such corporate surgery, be sure you have the leadership in place to have everyone cooperate and give of their best. Consider the words of a famous surgeon to his students: "When you begin to operate on a limb, remember that there is a human being attached to it."

Chapter 4

Hitting the Ground Running

One of the authors of this book has been an officer in the Parachute Regiment. He knows very well (and don't we all?) that you are not going to take the enormous risk of jumping out of a plane without knowing where you are likely to land or, at least, find yourself behind a trusted leader who knows.

The meaning of this book for you has been clearly explained—to ensure a steady stream of new products that will outstrip the competition. The different paths have already been identified. At a time when most people work in service industries: Take lawyers, they will aim at new specializations (litigation over internet offenses or—more generally—competition legislation).

Doctors' innovations will be in the more intangible realm of reputation—a reputation for being expert at certain specializations. They can take their share of credit for their part in the invention of so many new medical and surgical techniques such as innovations against pneumonia, and for keyhole surgery and the provision of artificial joints.

The transport operator has a more precise measure of efficiency—punctuality—but this impacts innovations such as new, more powerful, and safer equipment. New methods of compiling and presenting timetables are other possible innovations, especially for airlines, but also for buses, trains, and ships.

Shipping businesses frequently devise innovative tours as do coach companies and train systems. For freight, the switches from cargoes packed in cases or crates to bulk carrying in containers and on roll-on, roll-off ferries have resulted from the search for innovation.

These service professionals know well enough that their attempts at new product development will flop unless they are first meticulously thought out. It is a serious mistake to announce a new timetable in any transport undertaking unless you have the equipment to fulfill it.

Manufacturers and primary producers do not have the leisure to think at some depth, which is why committees, project groups, research departments, and even boards of directors are so urgently needed to do the thinking. This thinking must be strictly guided and controlled so that the objectives are met as quickly as possible and are not lost in forgetfulness or impossible fantasy (the difference between informal vision and "pie in the sky").

The message of this chapter is that once the thinking is over, the action needs to be fast. If one company is known to be working on an innovation, the odds are that several others are working frantically to get there first. So this is the moment to stop and ask the question: Is it best to be first or second? It depends on the circumstances. If the new product is a completely new invention toward which the market has not yet grown accustomed, it may be best to allow a competitor to be first. The competitor (company Y) will, then, help the potential customers to overcome their resistance to such an innovation, in effect to create the market, so long as a patent to prevent a second ever entering is not possible. This must have applied to most of the striking technical advances once considered luxuries but now considered essentials, which so changed twentieth-century lifestyles and working practices. The critical "new products" influencing lifestyles have included refrigerators, vacuum cleaners, personal computers, television sets, and many others. Working processes have been revolutionized by inventions under the general and overworked word "automation." In either case, the first company in the market has the enormous expense of persuading people that they do need and will enjoy the new product.

And yet, someone must be first. The company that occupies this tricky position must maintain its lead by making its own products obsolete before the competitors catch up and do so. This fight to maintain the lead is a common cradle for centers of excellence (Chapter 7).

THINKING AND JUMPING

This "thinking" will test the commitment of the project team. It will be working with strict deadlines but also with guidelines about the circumstances, within which the new product will be inaugurated at once or delayed to allow a competitor to open up the market. If the decision to be second is taken, there is still need of work to ensure the right response when the time comes.

In either case, patents will need to be taken out but, for the second company in, the technical staff need to ensure that there is a patentable technology which will differentiate the company's product from the first in without infringing its rights. If, on the other hand, the proposed development is an important change to an existing product, that is the time to jump.

Biscuit and cereal manufacturers are among those who, to the non-expert observer, always seem to be throwing up modified products to beat the competition and to increase their share of retailers' shelves without actually producing a radically new product—but the same principle can be applied over a wide range of consumer products. Let us assume it includes yours and look urgently for possibilities.

Let us assume, too, that all interested parties have reported favorably toward the scheme. A critical path must be worked out immediately by the project group with the agreement of marketing, production, and all the other functions concerned to be sure that all is completed by the date already identified by the project team as the most suitable day for the product launch.

How is that identification made? Consider the following list, surely some items on it will fit your company.

Items Identifying a Suitable Launch Date for a New Product

1. Is the product or service relevant to some national issue? Perhaps the emergence of a dangerous virus among farm animals or crops will spark off openings for new products for suppliers. These may be vaccines and other measures to cure or prevent the disease. For these you do need to be first in; you probably also need to be a large firm with sufficient resources to fund the research and production costs. A smaller firm can still find a niche: What about a consultancy to assist affected farmers to diversify the business? Alternatively, you may yourself diversify into specialist crops. Under most circumstances the small firm can look for components or subassemblies.

2. The product may fit an anniversary such as the ending of a war or civil action—nearly half the members of the United Nations can be seen to be in this position by a perceptive marketer.
3. The product may be launched as part of national celebrations or an anniversary.
4. The product may have special seasonal sales.

All promotions will be properly coordinated and dovetailed in so that the launch date in question is not overshadowed. If the Annual General Meeting is to be on that day, it will have to be postponed as will the chief executive's holiday; his presence will be required at the launch. All the resources of the company will be temporarily concentrated on the new product; "temporarily" because most innovations will not conflict with the mainstream business. When General Motors in the United States diversified into railway diesel locomotives, they continued to strive to maintain and enhance their place in the motor car industry, with great success.

All of a company's resources will be mobilized to ensure the most effective possible impact of the new (modified) product and this will hold good whatever the size of the firm. Some companies are notably adept at producing strong impacts on the market by product developments—waking up an otherwise sleepy sector with small changes which cause immense excitement.

In the late 1950s the gas industry was generally regarded as dying. It has not only survived since then but expanded enormously, mainly through innovations ranging from the coming of natural gas, through improved heat conservation techniques in industry to improved domestic appliances. Natural gas has largely replaced coal for generating electricity—still supreme among energy providers.

QUICK RESPONSE

The retail sector has needed to respond rapidly to new developments. A process that started with a simple and traditional exercise to cut costs and prices has led to a battle of the giants between large competing outfits in the United States and over most of Europe. A few niches have remained for the small shopkeepers which have been left to fight their corner over issues such as convenience and personal service.

BUT—there is a big but to that statement—the battle of the giants has developed into a struggle for power, a struggle which gives all the commercial advantages of semimonopoly to the winner: advantages which legislators have struggled to reduce; at the same time the balance of power between the producers and the wholesalers on the one hand and the retailers on the other has altered. If you are into retailing or into a sector that is like it, some hard thinking is needed about the role your company can play—about where the profitable outlets are. If you are locked into a niche, there is little scope for product innovation that is not dictated from the outside. Many small retailers in Britain have been kept alive by selling lottery tickets but this was not an innovation they sought. It arrived on their agenda by act of parliament and can leave the same way. Fortunately for them, this is unlikely to happen.

To the big retailers, the sale of lottery tickets must appear as an irrelevance, they need to keep in touch with the changing tastes of their customers. With every inch of shelf space costed in terms of cents (pennies) per hour, they need to find new products to match a demand appearing for tropical fruits but also nonfood items such as motoring equipment to match the demands of customers who have spent their holidays traveling abroad.

The big and growing retail firms also have to remember that a successful new product policy also requires an ability to cut out ruthlessly items which do not earn their keep in terms of dollars per square inch.

The need to watch the changing balance of power is reflected in the way that the larger retailers can force their suppliers to change their procedures by supplying goods by the means that is most suitable to new retailing methods. No longer can the suppliers get away with a sloppy delivery service or presentation; they need to "hit the ground running" in the way they respond to the supermarkets.

To improve their profitability and at the same time their reputation for quality, the large retailers press manufacturers to make goods under the retailer's own label. The quality of own label goods is as good as the branded products and costs just a little less to the consumer. A well-known United Kingdom retailer, Marks and Spencer, with a branch in every conurbation, sells nothing but goods bearing its own "St. Michael" label.

The following example is of a company that gradually raised the level of its technology but remained in the same industry.

SIDDALL AND HILTON LTD.

The Challenge of Maintaining Excellence

Founded at the end of the nineteenth century, Siddall and Hilton Ltd. is a family-owned group of companies, now in the fourth generation. It is managed by a multidisciplined board of directors, combining the established expertise of family members with vital additional skills from outside. Its products are mainly wire and spring related, ranging from wire coat hangers to adjustable hospital beds.

Two member companies, Siddall and Hilton Springs Ltd. and Chiltern Springs Ltd., which was acquired in 1997, manufacture bedding and upholstery springs. Redfearn Wire Products Ltd. makes coat hangers, container and industrial bucket handles, wire reels for welding wire, and some other wire sundries.

Siddall and Hilton Mesh Ltd. produces welded mesh and expanded metal products. It manufacturers several types of metal fencing, including high-security fencing as well as meshes for the construction industry and razor barbed wire.

Sidhil Ltd., strengthened by the acquisition of a strong competitor, Doherty Medical Ltd., is one of Europe's leading manufacturers of hospital and health care furniture and equipment. Each of these manufacturing subsidiaries is managed autonomously within group strategy. In order to support them without interference in operations, the parent company has recently established Siddall and Hilton Communications Ltd. to provide management services in the area of human resources, training, and individual development, keeping abreast with legislation affecting employees and other business improvement initiatives.

The group has completed a decade of expansion, involving sustained investment in innovation and acquisition. Each manufacturing subsidiary has its part to play in maintaining expansion and growth and in solving its own innovation problems to achieve agreed objectives. These are outlined in the following text.

Springs—Getting Productivity Up and Costs Down

Siddall and Hilton Springs and Chiltern Springs are in a highly competitive market. Bed and upholstery springs are today virtually commodity products, as they can be made so cheaply. To get ahead of competition, therefore, the companies have to find ways and means of raising productivity and product quality while reducing the cost of manufacture. They have formed a joint venture with a specialist company in Atlanta, Georgia, to research and develop a vastly improved method of coiling and assembling pocket springs. This will improve the strength and capability of springs while speeding up output at lower cost. Eventually this measure should enable them to offer their clientele better value for money. Development of the new machinery is on track but obtaining patent protection is proving a tough and lengthy process.

Coat Hangers—Ahead of the Market?

For many years Redfearn Wire Products Ltd. has been the leading manufacturer of wire coat hangers in Europe. In 1976 it developed a special lacquer coating process which created a smart bronze finish. Branded "Atlas Bronze," it became well established in Britain and other parts of Europe. The market is the laundry and dry cleaning industry. In recent years, however, the wire coat hanger business has been undermined. The company has been up against competition from one-person businesses which operate coat hanger machines in garages with hardly any overhead cost.

Meantime, a leading firm of dry cleaners set a new trend using plastic coat hangers. Although these cost six times more than wire products, the move made good marketing sense. A cleaned and pressed garment returned to the customer on a prestige hanger creates the assurance of a job well done. Furthermore, branded plastic coat hangers accumulating in a wardrobe are effective advertising.

In 1998 Redfearn decided to move into plastic coat hangers, leaping ahead of competitors by providing a hanger with a folding hook for easy packing into a suitcase. The folding hook also allows more economical packing for shipment—another cost advantage.

Redfearn invested in design and in commissioning a special injection-molding process to produce a lighter but stronger hanger at four times the normal rate of machine cycle.

Taking samples to the market, however, the company finds that its major customers are not yet ready to change to the folding hook design. This is surely a case of an innovation ahead of and not appreciated by the market.

A publicity program will be needed to get the new product into regular demand to reestablish the business as a leader in coat hanger manufacture.

Mesh—The Search for Additional Customer Benefits

A consumer durable product such as high-security, welded mesh, or expanded metal fencing, is more attractive to the customer if supplied with accessories to facilitate quick and easy use. Siddall and Hilton Mesh, therefore, sees its next innovative step as providing a system of posts, purchasable with the panels and crafted for easy erection. This is not an uncommon road to expansion. When the Phillips Screw Corporation of the United States invented the Posidriv screw, it asked Stanley Tools to develop a cheap screwdriver to handle it. Every time Gillette launches a new razor blade, it offers a razor to hold it.

Sidhil—The Need to Maintain Impetus

Sidhil Ltd. (formerly Sidhil Care) has traditionally supplied adjustable beds and other items of furniture and equipment to hospitals, community care establishments, and for private care use. In 1997 the company lost £500,000 ($750,000). By 1999 this was reversed into a profit of £750,000 ($1,125,000) through new and improved product development, and an overhaul of selling arrangements. Recovery was aided by the acquisition of a major competitor, Doherty Medical, which gave access into the general medical practitioners' market.

Under both the Sidhil and Doherty names, the company has modified the designs of its range of beds both for hospital and community care use. For example, under the Sidhil label, the company has developed an electrically operated "Independence" ward bed with several new beneficial features. These include a new configuration of adjustable bed panels to prevent patients who are in a full or semi sitting-up position from sliding down the bed. It has two control handsets, one for the patient, the other for the caregiver that can override the former. The bed runs on special nonmarking castors.

Sidhil has also developed two new lightweight adjustable beds for use in the home or in community care establishments. Branded the "Freedom" and the "Millennium" beds, both can be easily assembled by one person, even the patient. They are attractively styled.

An attractive style is also the main feature of Sidhil's new "Signature" range of furniture for offices of general practitioners. This furniture consists of examination couches, desks, cabinets, and cupboards. All are elegantly designed to create a far more homely and less clinical ambience in the surgery, even though some of the pieces have stainless steel tops.

In addition, the company launched its "Inspiration" child's cot, which while cheerful in appearance, can be adjusted in any direction. Its variations include height, incline of the bed panel, and lowering of all four sides singly or together. In overhauling its range of products, the company has designed them for lightweight and streamlined appearance, as well as optimizing the use of common components, drastically reducing the former inventory of thousands of different slow moving parts.

The replacement of its territorial sales agents by a trained field sales force has been a substantial aid to the company's achievement of increased profitable volume.

Sidhil now faces the challenge of maintaining its rate of growth. This will be achieved by pressing on with more new product development and by combining such innovation with penetration into new market segments in the medical and health care fields. It also needs to expand its profitable share of traditional markets.

Center(s) of Excellence?

In the Siddall and Hilton Group, the responsibility for successful innovation rests firmly on the shoulders of the group chief executive. Although each subsidiary is managed autonomously, he must provide directors with leadership, help, and advice to ensure achievement of their objectives.

Part of this help and advice must involve making available a center or centers of excellence. For this need, the CEO has recruited an experienced group director of research and development.

If the chief executive agrees to all subsidiaries setting up their own center of excellence, the advantage would be that each could concentrate on its own specialities such as plastics for coat hangers, wire for springs, wire for mesh, or lightweight materials for hospital beds. The disadvantage would be the enormous cost.

If the CEO sets up one center of excellence for the entire group, the advantage would be in cost savings, but could all specialities be adequately covered under one roof? Another point the CEO raises is, if a center is located nearer to one company than to another, would the more distant business be inclined not to make full use of it? The problem is still being studied, and it would not be appropriate to try to make any forecast at present.

One (hopefully prudent) principle is that if a subsidiary can maintain profitable performance, has an innovation plan worthy of investment, and can contribute from its profits toward its own center, then it should establish a center in its own right. If a subsidiary can evidence such overwhelming promise of successful innovation, then its own center should be financed from group funds regardless of its past profitability record.

Siddall and Hilton could consider Sidhil supplying hospitals, general practitioners (physicians), and community care establishments and could possibly create its own center from its profits to ensure further expansion.

Aside from Sidhil, the remaining subsidiaries concerned with wire-related products could use a shared center of excellence. If, however, in later years Redfearn moves successfully into plastic products, it could eventually need a center of excellence to specialize in plastic materials and manufacturing techniques.

If not tightly controlled, product innovation can consume money at an alarming rate. In Siddall and Hilton, the group chief executive, aided by the group director of research and development, must make centers of excellence available to all the manufacturing subsidiaries as financially sound as possible.

Many readers may be facing this problem. Make sure that the work of everyone employed in a center of excellence is measurable. The excellence they produce must be evidenced by the continuous flow of successful new products, all developed within agreed financial budgets.

Redfearn's challenge in rebuilding its position in the coat-hanger market suggests that:

- No product is too mundane to be the object of innovative thinking. Who would have thought that an article so simple as a coat-hanger would call for so much investment for change?
- It is perilous to lose touch with the development of new materials with innovative applications in your industry sector. Competitors are defeated by companies with early knowledge of the development of new materials.
- It is even more dangerous to lose touch with innovative thinking among your customers.
- Guaranteed availability is always worth the cost to keep customers loyal.
- Subcontracting part of the manufacturing process is needed when speed to market is essential. In this case the objective is leap-frogging ahead of competitors.
- In addition, in planning new hi-tech products, credibility is crucial. Do not usually depart too far from products for which the company already has a reputation.

COMMUNICATIONS

Much of this chapter has been concerned with retailing, which has provided most of the examples so far, but speed has proved vital to every sector of business. Thus one small British engineering company (BHE Services [Bolton] Ltd.) ensured its place among its competitors by installing a state-of-the-art communications system, allowing it to alert customers (and its own staff) of innovations important for its business in the least possible time.

Sense of Urgency

This is all too often lacking, and constant pressure from management, and higher management, is needed to avoid delays down the chain. An excellent example may be found in *Modern Railways* for December 2000. The article discussed an accident near the southern end of the East Coast main line in Britain in November of that year, in which four people were killed. Within three weeks the line had not been reopened. The article referred to another accident in 1965 on the same stretch of line just after midnight in which five people were killed. On this occasion the line was reopened that evening. Neither of these accidents had anything to do with new product development but both concerned the need to recruit people who showed an adequate sense of urgency in an emergency.

What Have We Learned from This Chapter?

The answer is timing, along with a need for speed, *once the decision is made,* but also need for *thought* before the decision is made.

To process the "thought" quickly enough, some processing body is required, call it a committee, "project group," "working party," or what you will; it must work with a schedule that will leave the competition far behind.

Chapter 5

Ideas, Ideas, Ideas

Ours is the only country deliberately founded on a good idea.

Thom Gunn on the United States

You may well wonder what inspired such complacent patriotism, but you will know that all profitable developments spring from good ideas and that ideas spring from people; they do not grow in the ground like brussels sprouts. This is illustrated by the following hypothetical conversation in an anonymous company.

"Chief, I have a good idea. What about a high-speed laser printer at about the price of an ordinary dot matrix?"

"Hang on a minute, James. From what dark mental dungeon do you conjure up a low cost laser?"

The man addressed as "chief" was silent for a few minutes. He spent a lot of time and emotional energy trying to bring out new ideas from his staff and James was one who always responded but repeatedly put forward bright but obviously unprofitable ideas; in this case he saw the possibilities and he did not want to dam the suggestions flood. James had obviously done some homework—he was soon to learn how much—and the firm's last laser printer had stood up well in an extremely competitive market. That would have given them credibility in the marketplace while the research department was already forecasting that the cost could be driven down.

"How much homework have you done, James?"

"I've talked to research and they've nearly reached a low cost machine that could wipe the market. Give it a whirl, chief." He spoke with an enthusiastic urgency signaling that he really believed in the proposition. "I've done all the calculations, everything that you keep telling us to do."

"OK, let's see the proposal."

That story represents just one way in which a new idea may come into the system. Look at the following options.

1. An idea can come from a management group (that is to say inside the firm) after much battling by the leader to bring it to fruition. In this case the leader was frustrated that he so often had to shoot down the ideas when they came on the grounds of "unprofitability," so he was glad to find a suggestion with evidence indicating that further investigation would be worthwhile.
2. The idea was for a modification of an existing product to sell at a new price level.

So what other possibilities are there?

The idea may come from a customer, perhaps commenting to a sales representative. It may also come from other sources outside the firm through, for example, the monitoring of markets and especially of competitors or the trade press or again as a result of seminars to which managers are sent to improve their performance in general and to pick up ideas in particular. Or again, a thoughtful employee may have studied the catalogs of computer peripheral stores to find something a firm could handle.

Whatever the source, the idea will be picked up by an individual and, if judged likely to be successful, eventually passed to a product development committee. It will then be examined, tested, and given a rating. There will be a formal, calculated rating of anticipated return, as well as an informal rating of enthusiasm and drive. The formal ratings are needed to convince the city, but the success of the project will depend on the informal ratings coming from individuals whether the "chief" or "James" or any other member of the team are prepared to put heads on the block to drive the project through. That is where the ideas side comes in—and it won't come if James is shot down in flames every time he attempts to respond to the pressure for new ideas.

Never underestimate the number of sources; wherever there are people there are ideas. You may say, "Not so with our firm; they're a bunch of zombies without a thought in their heads." To that we reply, "If that is true, you need to reexamine your recruitment and your training methods," after reexamining yourselves, of course.

All new products represent a risk that has to be minimized. For this reason, minor modifications of existing products are likely to be preferred to a move into a completely new product or a new market. Better (more profitable) to build on an existing reputation than to look for a new one. Sometimes a brilliant change of course is a 100 percent success. Otherwise let us breathe new life into a traditional one, in which the business has a reputation for excellence.

In either case, there are numerous sources of ideas. The population of the world is growing toward the six billion mark, and many of them could have ideas that would help your company. Most companies prefer to look inside first and canvas all the insiders for ideas. In some large firms generous payments are made for ideas that work.

A press report (*Financial Times,* July 16, 1997) showed how two service companies had improved their performance rapidly after putting employee ideas into practice, both through innovative practices. One firm mentioned was Gardner Merchant (caterers to steel and car workers as well as to staff and pupils at Eton College). The firm also organizes meetings to spread innovative ideas across its world. The other company—Going Places—is also an international service company.

Take companies of solicitors or accountants where new legislation provides opportunities for products that help existing or future clients to take into account the effects of new legislation.

If most ideas are unearthed from inside the company, the number of resources that can be tapped from outside are limitless, to such an extent that possibilities must be limited by some strict criteria that ensure time is not wasted on too many nonstarters. However, first we ask ourselves: Where else do ideas come from?

Some companies set limits to innovative ideas. For example, Lord Hanson, a well-known international entrepreneur, restricts his companies' activities to products which are essential, while a manufacturer of precious metal products is likely to resist getting into the rat race of low cost and low price synthetics.

IDEAS FROM WITHIN THE BUSINESS

"Necessity is the mother of invention." Motivating people to come up with ideas involves keeping them informed of the company's goals, what is needed to achieve these goals, and how they can help. People should be updated on problems and be asked to make suggestions for solving them. In short, tell them the *necessity* and encourage them to *invent*.

This is achieved by planned briefing meetings at say, two-week intervals throughout the business. Directors will hold a meeting to brief managers; each manager will have his or her meeting to brief supervisors and foremen. They, in turn, will brief other employees.

The following is an example of foreman Joe briefing his team of workers at a cherry canning factory. "In six weeks time we have to begin preparing Christmas orders. This year the demand is bigger than ever. Last year we had a log jam in labeling; labels were coming off as cans went into cartons. All summer we've been running trials with instant adhesives, but these are so sensitive they get stuck on the sides of the labeling machine."

"Joe," says Harry, "my wife Hannah works in a cigarette factory; she tells me the cigarette-making machines shoot a blast of hot air on the gum line as the two sides of the paper are stuck together. What about running the cans quickly through a hot drying compartment between labeling and cartoning?"

"Thank you, Harry," replies Joe. "Would you like to sketch out that idea and work out at what point on the line we could fix it? In the meantime, I'll tell Mr. Carruthers [Department Head] about it. Before we break up, ladies and gentlemen, I have another matter to bring to your attention: The directors are finding that the canned cherry business is too seasonal. Either we have to find ways and means of persuading people to buy them *all* the year round, or we've got to can something else to bolster the slack season. We can't just can anything, because many fruits such as pineapples and peaches are dominated by Del Monte and the big boys. The company needs to come up with something new. Your suggestions would be most welcome."

IDEAS FROM OUTSIDE THE BUSINESS

The art of generating ideas from outside the business is to ask customers, suppliers, advisers, and all people concerned with the business what their problems are and then consider how the company can help.

The famous Gripple device, which fastens miles of fence wire all over the world, was conceived by the managing director listening to a user of his wire. "Boyo, your wire is fine" said a user, a Welsh farmer, "but I get so sick of all the turning and twisting needed to fasten it to fence posts." The wire manufacturing company then started work on inventing a device to satisfy the need for an easy, instant method for joining strands of wire to posts and to each other. Today the company no longer makes wire; it concentrates all its resources on improving the Gripple wire-joining device.

Sources of Inspiration

Start with the local library—the company library if there is one—and set the Jameses of the company the task of ferreting around, but not indefinitely. You are unlikely to say, "OK, James, off to the city library and don't come back until you have been inspired with a new idea that our company could develop." Instead, you might say, "OK, James, off to the city library and report for work tomorrow morning with six new ideas worth assessing by our Product Development Committee." With a couple of Jameses in the firm (and they should not be too difficult to recruit), you will never be short of ideas for new products. But this should not stop at libraries. What about museums?

Even an old piece of apparatus may produce ideas that can quickly be adapted to new product development. For example, a wire drawer walked into an industrial museum and studied some of the earliest wire drawing equipment. He then built a completely new machine using the oldest methods but driven by solid-state electronics instead of water, steam, or electric motors. It has been said, indeed, that the sale of licenses for reproducing their goods has been a remunerative venture for museums such as the Victoria and Albert and the British Museum. To go back further still, binary arithmetic—the basis of modern computer technology—was discovered by the ancient Greek philosophers. Incidentally, the "lost wax" method of precision metal castings, for example airplane parts and artificial hips, can be seen in 2,000 year-old examples in the National Museum in Athens. For the sharp-sighted, the world (including your little piece of it) is full of suggestions for developments waiting to happen.

Readers of this book are unlikely to be in a position that searches libraries and museums—although they may have been once—rather they will be thinking up briefings for the searchers; common sense will tell them that what you put in, you get out; ill-briefed searchers are likely to disappoint themselves and you.

Another source of ideas is the competition. A watch over what the competitors are up to is not only likely to provide a benchmark to test new developments. Say, if the competitors can do that, we can do it better. The ultimate disgrace is to leave a gap in the market that can be filled easily and profitably.

STRATEGIC ALLIANCES

While the distinction between external and internal sources of ideas for new product development is an illuminating way of analyzing the methods of obtaining new ideas, there is a way which can prove a more prolific source than either; that is by agreement with another company for the sharing of ideas. The agreement, which is used by large and small companies, can take a number of forms, but expert legal advice is always essential to ensure that it is unlikely to be considered an illegal restraint of trade.

The most common form of agreement, and the most relevant to small and medium-sized companies without the resources to buy the proposed partner, is the *joint venture*. Once the problem of "restraint of trade" has been overcome, there are a number of other issues to take into account. The most important is to ensure that each partner is likely to be satisfied that it is able to realize its objectives in setting up the venture. This is achieved by setting up a high level board recruited from articulate representatives of each company. The partner which is seeking to increase its flow of new products must be able to satisfy its search, while the other partner must be satisfied that it is receiving adequate remuneration for its products and, in particular, the research involved in developing them. The most common complaint about joint ventures is couched in terms such as: "We put in all the resources but our partner takes half of the revenue." Safeguards against that perception are needed during the preparatory work as well as the wording of the final contract.

Another means of acquiring new products is through a licensing agreement or management contract. These are similar arrangements but, in the case of a basic licensing agreement, technical information and related patents are transferred between two companies; in the case of the management contract relevant management techniques are transferred for a fee at the same time. Indeed the total management of the project may be undertaken by the licensor. Circumspection is found to be necessary because the word "management" in management contract is unacceptable in some countries; it is held to be an insult to local management abilities.

A similar concept is known as a *franchising agreement.* While the words are often used loosely and interchangeably, the basic franchise is the transfer of a body of commercial knowledge along with a product. This technique is frequently used in service industries such as hospitality and tourism. Hotel chains have increased their geographical range with a portfolio of different arrangements: one hotel may be operated by a joint venture, another a management contract, and yet another a franchise arrangement.

The franchising arrangement usually passes to the franchisee trademarks, brand names, training, and marketing, as well as other commercial techniques. Apart from the trademarks, most of the commercial knowledge is not controlled by law as is the patent in a licensing agreement. In spite of this, franchising is a fast-expanding technique which is relevant to the expansion of the service industries.

On the manufacturing side, there is manufacture under contract which will not always produce a new product; there is also the turnkey contract which provides for the operation of a new facility once built. This will require a long time lead but is otherwise likely to offer a new product. After deciding which products would lead most surely toward a company's strategic aims, a search should be set up to identify firms suitable for takeover, merger, or the negotiation of a strategic alliance.

ENVIRONMENTALLY FRIENDLY PRODUCTS

A series of meetings, the first in Rio and the second in Kyoto (in 1997) and the third in Amsterdam (in 2000) have been aimed at stimulating panic over environmental issues, even if we see more panic than action on the part of governments. The opportunities offered have already been recognized by some firms which have been able to market environmentally friendly products and machinery for which the market is expanding rapidly. An example described in *Business*

North West, August 1997, is that of James Briggs, a Lancashire (England)-based concern that has been making chemicals and polishes since 1830. As their product range has spread into specialist waxes and aerosols, the firm has learned how many of the traditional ingredients of these products are damaging to the environment and have devoted much attention to producing more environmentally friendly options. This is a clear example of a diversification that takes advantage of a shift in the market place.

While polishes and chemicals are aimed at both consumer and business markets, a firm that emphasizes ever higher quality in industrial accessories is Schwer Fittings Ltd. of Warrington, Cheshire (England). This company has demonstrated that ever-closer concentration on customer needs generates new ideas in a market that is both specialist and demanding. Ever more accurate measurements are required.

What Have We Learned from This Chapter?

- To keep exploring every avenue for collecting new ideas originating from inside and outside the company.
- To ensure, so far as possible, that new ideas are encouraged and their sources are not destroyed as far as their usefulness to our company is concerned.
- Keep everyone in the business informed of the *necessities* to achieve goals and overcome problems and they will surely *invent* through those ideas and suggestions.
- A company is needed in which the enthusiastic search for new ideas is always present and is not discouraged (see also Chapter 11).

Chapter 6

Product Development: Corporate Strategy

Let us begin this chapter with a statement of the obvious: product development cannot ignore a general statement of the corporate strategy of which it is part.

For instance, assume our corporate strategy is to service the top end of the market. No proposal to invest in cheap, more popular, products just to chalk up an innovation can be entertained. In practice this does not appear so obvious as it seems when you say it. A firm making electric light bulbs for the expensive end of the market once discovered that a foreign subsidiary had begun to make cheap bulbs without any guarantee of length of life with the intention of boosting the subsidiary's profit.

And the result? The subsidiary's profit did, indeed, receive a temporary boost, but worldwide the company lost out. Customers were confused; the retail outlets no longer knew where to place the bulbs on their shelves and the buyer no longer knew what to expect, a reminder that a move in one market soon affects others.

In this case, the innovation not only produced permanent damage to the company's reputation and hence its sales, the company was left frantically trying to restore its position in the market. The word "frantically" is interesting. Technically it can only be applied to individuals. Used of companies, it means that all too much management time is absorbed in sorting out a problem that should never have existed. A strategy to service "only the top end of the market" is costly to restore once broken.

The argument so far is summarized by the need when dealing with consumer products to avoid innovation that leads to a different market sector. Of course, as with all management principles, this does not apply universally. Parallel products are practical possibilities. For instance, it has been said of Mitsubishi that when, with typical farsightedness, the company's managers foresaw a major crisis in ship-building, they were able to transfer successful technology gradually into other heavy products in machinery or transportation. This is an instance of where the corporate planning needs sufficient breadth to encompass such repositioning. That is the other side of the coin, you might well argue. On the one side, the planning must not be so flexible that it allows shifts of activity into products that destroy a firm's hard-won reputation; on the other it must not be so inflexible as to make profitable innovation all but impossible. An example of a profitable move by a company out of products for which it was well-known has been Saab, the Swedish aircraft company, which made a successful move into cars; another example, also into cars, was Honda's move from motorcycles.

No one expects a middle- or small-sized company (SME) to make such drastic changes of product line as Mitsubishi (Mitsubishi has entered the British rail equipment market) *or* Saab, a company which has changed from aircraft to cars. The company would, indeed, be ill-advised to try. Delusions of grandeur are seldom profitable, but the principle of diversification along related technologies is always worth a glance. The expression "lateral thinking" has been brought into management thought—a valuable expression, but it can call into question the compatibility between innovation and strategy.

The evaluation of a proposal needs to include the question: Does it fit with or contradict the positioning of our long-range strategy? Or is the opportunity so great and promising that our strategy must be changed?

That question has already been answered in part, but it raises other pressing questions about planning and implementation—not just whether this proposal fits with or contradicts our strategy. Does the proposal arise from the strategy? How vigilant is this company in looking out for targets that progress its strategic objectives, or avoiding those that conflict with them?

The example of Mitsubishi seems to contradict the earlier statement about fitting with the corporation's long-term plans, although the strategy statement might well include something along the lines of "lateral thinking," a subject which now comes up at almost every reputable executive seminar, expressed in such words as: "the search for new products will encompass opportunities in related industries which use relevant technologies and which are saleable in similar markets." In general, the search requires a company with sufficient resources to sustain the research along with any recommendations that result. There is usually scope for the further exploiting of existing skills or experience.

To incorporate these questions into a board's already overcrowded agenda is yet another powerful stimulus to innovation, although most executives discover that this is not the way things happen. To keep a member of staff on the watch all the time is really to make a full-time job out of an activity which should find a place in every manager's job description. While some members of the staff will be especially vigilant, all will be expected to shout when they see an opportunity for launching a new product on the market, a product which can be expected to show a profit without proving too demanding on the company's resources. Gaps in the market do not appear casually; they appear because someone has been actively looking for them.

The "relentless thrust" (see Chapter 1) is meant to drive everyone, but they will be expected to remain flexible.

Flexibility does not have to mean aimlessness. It does mean strong leadership, which asks of any proposal how it fits with the route guide. Does it take the company along a predetermined route or is it confusing the landmarks? The "thrust" needs to be guided as well as "relentless."

THE CORPORATE STRATEGY: TARGETS

The objectives defined by the strategy will include the target market (quality and price), the target return on investment and stockholders' funds, and quality of staff (recruitment and training). (See our book on corporate strategy, *The Visionary Executive*, Cambridge 1997.) These objectives will need to be matched by the new product policies.

The last paragraph could be said to introduce an element of lateral thinking into the issue of corporate strategy, although we assume that this is likely to be there already. The target market and the target return on investment can be taken for granted, the need for staff matching the demands that our services still make on them, and, when necessary, a training program to bring them up to the mark.

In drafting its corporate strategy, a company (large or small) will spend much time fixing the targets which will be its guidelines for ever after. Some of these targets will be unstated, taken for granted as part of the purpose in founding the company. This will apply especially to the fundamental target from which the others will be derived: positioning in the marketplace with which this chapter opened.

It will be generally known that product X (or service Y) is aimed at the expensive, scarce end of the market and is to be generally described as "up-market." Efforts will be made frequently to prevent the dilution of the up-market image, which is a fundamental part of the product or service itself. It is widely believed indeed that innovation is most effectively launched up-market. Once the reputation is established, it may be possible to cater for a cheaper mass market which will normally lie behind—however much caution is used in doing so. Such a move has been successfully demonstrated by quality carmakers who find themselves able to produce a smaller, cheaper model without ruining their image. Both Volvo and Jaguar have discovered this possibility of producing a smaller model, which benefits from the reputation of the established models without diluting the image so painstakingly established.

If the company will sternly safeguard itself against wrecking a hard-won image for satisfying the discriminating customer/client, this safeguard will help to preserve another target, *return on investment*. This is another vital target in any formulation of strategy, one which emphasizes the long-term nature of strategic planning. We are looking to a tomorrow fraught with numerous unknowns when we identify a return on investment calculation based on as many foreseeable characteristics as possible. That is the nature of target setting, a nature which is particularly well illustrated in the return on investment equation but applies also to other targets as well.

No one knows, for instance, the likely problems in hiring and retaining staff into the long-term future but a company's reputation will depend on policies that allow for many unknowns and yet can somehow be made to succeed. Innovation policies will always include an element of a gamble. The uncertainties can be reduced but never abolished.

INTERNATIONAL ALLIANCES

A major element in corporate strategy is the international alliance. Two or more companies join in a joint venture or merger to promote the business of each in tackling vicious international competition. An example of this is Mossley Spinning in Greater Manchester (England) (mentioned in *Business North West,* December 1997), which formed an alliance with a French textile company nearly seventy years ago. This alliance has been through many changes to arrive at a powerful force in the textile world with sales approaching £130m ($165m), and employees exceeding 1,000. This is a splendid example of how international collaboration in a threatened industry, along with sensitivity to customers in the big stores, has sustained a powerful unit in a threatened industry. Next time you wear that special sweater (if global warming hasn't made it redundant!) remember that international effort over many years has kept a tiny part of the once-mighty textile industry thriving.

In sum, let us repeat two statements.

A shift in one market will have repercussions in others.

Corporate planning must be flexible enough to allow major shifts without allowing moves into markets that will destroy a firm's hard-won reputation.

Now let us examine one fictitious company, a joint venture in Europe. This is a completely fictitious company made up of the experiences of several real companies that the writer has encountered. It would be impossible to produce an example of the problem of a contradiction between strategy and practice using a real company; this business sector is so limited in numbers of members that the company would be readily identifiable and the account would be vetoed because inevitably it would be seen as unfair to some employees. The names used here are Lifelong Products Plc. in Britain, Lifelong Products Inc. in the United States, and Products pour Toute la Vie Sa in France and Switzerland. The nationalities are *not* significant; they are given here to make the account appear more realistic.

A PHARMACEUTICAL COMPANY: LIFELONG

During the 1990s, Lifelong set up a company council consisting of five senior executives from the Swiss head office and the chief executives of each of the eighteen foreign subsidiaries. This council had spent five years working out a strategic plan expected to guide the company for the next thirty years.

The pharmaceutical industry is divided into two parts. There are the medical products that are usually not for direct sale to the public (the so-called "ethical" pharmaceuticals) and are researched at length and designed to treat specific ailments. This part incurs the biggest risks when a long period of expensive research either produces no results or is overtaken by a competitor. The biggest profits are also made in the medical subsector because the market is willing to pay a high price for a valuable treatment.

The other subsector of the industry consists of the production of common, usually branded, products which are sold over the counter in pharmacies and provide the bulk of the business in those shops. This is a high turnover, low margin sector. One problem for the sales forces is the identification of the customer. For Britain, the United States, and other countries with highly developed regulations concerning the purchase of medical pharmaceuticals, the customer is not the person who places the order but the doctor who gives the instruction about which pharmaceutical to order and then issues prescribing details to patients (or their physicians). Some doctor, somewhere in the system, is normally responsible for the important purchasing decisions. The situation may be more complicated in the large hospital, although the skilled sales representative can usually track down the significant decision maker—a skill they are proud of and which is very profitable to the company.

The search for the customer is even more complicated with over-the-counter products. Purchases are made by members of the public toward whom promotions are launched but, in the final buying decision, availability and presentation are likely to be just as important. Large retailing groups will have their own purchasing departments as will the wholesalers who supply the smaller retailers. Their attitudes along with the margins available and reputations of the firms involved will help to determine sales.

Head office managers argued that the future of the company was entirely in medical pharmaceuticals and that the other product units should be sold off to raise funds for a rapid expansion in medicines. One advantage of this, it was argued, was that they would be better able to recruit top scientists to develop new pharmaceuticals, thus minimizing the risk in a business that was recognized to be high in risks combined with high rewards.

Most of the representatives from the wealthier countries agreed with this view but some from the poorer nations disagreed, arguing that medical drugs were too expensive for their countries and extremely difficult to sell there. They had little incentive to contribute toward the progress of a company that concentrated on medical drugs since their countries did not produce sufficiently advanced science.

After much debate it was decided that after ten years the company would concentrate on medical drugs and phase out the over-the-counter products. This was eventually agreed to by all the participants, although reluctantly by some.

The sales representatives in all the subsidiaries were enthusiastic about the result. This included those employed by subsidiaries in the poorer countries who had negotiated for themselves some rights to manipulate the pricing structure when selling in those countries. They had established good relations with the senior medical authorities in those countries and knew how to manipulate the system.

One further detail about the company: Research was not concentrated, as is usual, in one large unit, but was spread among three which were in constant communication through online links. The result was that those three subsidiaries had a stake in the research and an incentive to push it forward while it drew on the scientists, a scarce resource; all three retained the facility of advertising internationally for staff.

The next development occurred three years into the ten-year period when the research unit came up with a new product that caused great excitement. It was assumed that this new product, a cough cure, would sell brilliantly over pharmacists' counters. Those who argued that developing this product contradicted their company's long-term strategic plan were ridiculed and called "sticks-in-the-mud" with no practical business sense. The new over-the-counter product was produced and did sell well, as expected, but caused a long-term slump in all other company products. The sales forces were confused and demoralized. Where was their focus supposed to be?

The reader may well advise them on an answer to the question.

To conclude this chapter, the message is: The offer you can't refuse may turn out to be a killer.

PART III:
CENTERS OF EXCELLENCE

Credibility is given to new product development if the innovator company already has a reputation in the marketplace for excellence. We hardly need to be reminded that this reputation is not acquired overnight. It comes as a result of a package of measures promoted over the years; it (the reputation) is also easily lost by carelessness within the company or overshadowed by a rising star among its competitors.

So what do we mean by a center of excellence? We mean the end of a process which goes through the following stages:

1. Determine the niche into which a "center of excellence" could be fitted. This will vary with the kind of business.
2. Assess the main competitors for that niche and where their strengths lie.
3. Work out the personal approach required from all levels of staff. This varies from absolute adherence to quality standards in the manufacturing industry to unfailing patience and willingness to humor the difficult customer in a service industry even if a willingness to bend the rules slightly is required. Pleasing the customer even at the expense of a slight infringement of the rules is one of the subtle issues involved in excellence in the service industries. Anyone deeply imbued with bureaucratic nonsense like "if we do it for one, we'll have to do it for all" is disqualified from managing a center of excellence.
4. In keeping with the main theme of this book, it must be said that a center of excellence is a center of people who are excellent at the job in hand.

5. Progress toward acquiring a reputation for excellence is a package—if we may use such an overworked word—of measures which combine to promote the required reputation. Look back at the list of contents at the beginning of this book to find a list of subjects that are included in the package.

6. Center of excellence does not mean that we take at face value the numerous claims that are made these days by organizations or units claiming to be such. A center of excellence must be recognized by outsiders.

Each of the chapters in this part covers a subject which could be a book on its own. The subjects are considered as necessary parts both of new product development and of centers of excellence—to which they are all related. These are:

Professionalism

A powerful impetus to centers of excellence has come through the rapid expansion of management education in recent years. This impetus usually stems from an emphasis on the need for a greater standard of professionalism among managers.

It is not always easy to understand the meaning of the word "professionalism." To many, it expresses an aim to match the claims of other so-called professions which have standards and regulations backed by organizations that enforce them, such as accountants and lawyers.

In an evident attempt to match the Hippocratic oath of the doctor, a management education institution in India demands of its successful students that they take a "management oath." This is summarized in the following text.

A winner of a Management Diploma at the Institute of Technology at Ghazabiad undertakes to practice all the tenets of good governance.

As we said of a center of excellence, a professional is one who is recognized by others.

Chapter 7 has examples that show that the expression "centers of excellence" can be used by more than one type of organization by, for instance: (1) a company center for supplies to other units of the company; (2) a business sector center, a striking contribution to the sector; (3) a company unit that is well above the norm; (4) a national or any international center of excellence.

Apart from number one (an in-company center), all rest on outside recognition of a company's achievements. Numbers 3 and 4, geographically defined, raise other interesting questions. A "world beater" indicates a reputation that has been built up probably through generations of careful attention to detail. Between the "international" center and the "national" there are other possibilities such as regional (continental) centers of excellence. Of all these types, the most sought after are the internal, in-company centers of excellence and the international. The subject is explored in Chapter 7 through a series of brief examples.

Chapter 7

Centers of Excellence

The rule by which he had always lived was that the best would have to do until something better came along.

P. G. Wodehouse

Did you read the introduction to Part III carefully? If so you may well have been left wondering what more was left to say about the centers of excellence? This chapter will expand on the concept.

A CENTER OF EXCELLENCE IN A SERVICE COMPANY: INSIGHT MONITORING

Imagine a fast-moving conveyor belt shifting hundreds of tons of coal per hour in a colliery. If it breaks down, the pit loses productivity at the rate of £20,000 ($30,000) per coal face feeding the belt for each hour needed to repair the fault. One conveyor will often move coal from several coal faces. It is imperative to take all reasonable steps to prevent stoppages.

The most common reasons for breakdowns are in bearings, motors, and gear boxes. Go all out to organize the early detection of signs of failure and to replace components during routine maintenance and down-time, rather than suffer expensive breakdowns *(predictive maintenance)*.

Before 1989, Alan Smith, a qualified engineer, had been employed by British Coal as a senior deputy engineer. He was employed in predictive maintenance in a colliery. Realizing that in the late 1980s the coal industry was shrinking (and reducing his prospects of promotion) he applied for early retirement and invested his payoff in financing and equipping his own predictive maintenance business: Insight Monitoring Services. His business mission was to provide this expertise to British Coal and other industries for which high machine availability and reliability were essential.

The initial equipment was the same as used in a British coal mine—two shock pulse monitoring meters together with one oil debris monitor for the ferrous testing of oil samples. He worked from his home for six months while his wife kept records and conducted correspondence on a primitive Commodore 64 computer. At that time there were two main methods of predicting the approaching collapse or malfunction of a component on a running machine.

The first was to listen to and record the normal vibrations while recording also their numerical values. This was written out by hand before the figures were plotted into a simple computer program. Afterward further readings would be taken at intervals and these would be compared with the original norm to detect irregularities and trend deviations.

The second was the analysis of oil samples from the main part of the sump to search for traces of eroding components. In September 1991 the company enhanced its capability by acquiring equipment for checking vibration. This enabled the feeding of vibration figures directly into the computer without any hand recording and with greater accuracy.

From 1989 through 1992, Insight Monitoring enjoyed a succession of predictive maintenance assignments with British Coal. This did not leave Alan Smith with any cause for complacency. On the contrary, he engaged a second engineer to allow him time to investigate his prospects in industries other than coal. By the end of 1992, the company had gained a foothold in cement making, rolling mills, wire drawing, and the frozen food industries.

Insight Monitoring was not having it all its own way. It was up against larger and better financed competitors, but Alan Smith held his own by establishing criteria of excellence which others had difficulty in matching. He placed no reliance on advertising or public relations activities but concentrated on establishing the business as a center of excellence in predictive maintenance. This involved long hours spent analyzing the readings of vibrations taken from machines so that findings would be reported to clients within forty-eight hours, even more quickly if a fault were discovered to be dangerously imminent. Clients were asked to take remedial action as quickly as demanded by the degree of urgency of the identified defect—how critical it was for further production.

In addition to the importance of the time factor, the readings have to be recorded clearly and the interpretation must be accurate in minute detail. The same high standards are maintained in oil analysis as in the electronic recording and analysis of vibrations. Hand in glove with performance excellence, it has been necessary to update and upgrade equipment to undertake a greater volume of work without lowering the operating standards.

Within the business shock pulse monitoring meters have been superseded by FFT (Fast Fourier Transform) data collectors which perform with greater speed and accuracy. By 1998 the company was moving into the then-latest development of collection technology—in the newest generation of FFT data collectors. The computers and the software have been continuously updated in step with the improved data collection capability.

Recently, through an associated company, the prognostic techniques have been extended into thermal imaging to predict malfunction through the sensing of abnormal heat. This technique detects electrical faults, insulation faults, and water leakage.

One problem for Insight Monitoring has been lack of understanding among client staff. As a result it has been policy to provide training for clients' personnel to understand the techniques being used in their establishments. This enables them to take the fullest possible advantage from Insights' services. For example, some clients today can send vibration readings by modem and telephone line from their machines directly to the computers in Insight's base office.

In 1996 Insight Monitoring suffered a serious blow. Coal Investments, which had taken over pits from British Coal, went into liquidation. It owed Insight a large sum of money which was earmarked for payment of loans from the bank and British Coal Enterprises. The effects of the loss of payment for work done was exacerbated by the cancellation of future work which had been scheduled by Coal Investments before it collapsed. The business rode out this crisis by tightening its belt in every aspect, except the standard of excellent service, which was fully maintained, and it held on to the team of highly trained staff.

From Coal to Food

By 1998 the company no longer operated in what was left of the coal industry. The workload in that industry had become out of all proportion to the very low financial reward. The clientele has since become more broadly based and more valuable than ever before. Insight Monitoring now serves a variety of industries. It monitors the pumps and motors that feed the extruders in a pasta factory, which provides the entire needs for the recipe dishes of a countrywide supermarket chain. Likewise it services the machinery feeding the extruders of a plastics factory. A client in the frozen food industry needs to monitor freezer compressors and chocolate conching machines. (In the chocolate manufacturing industry, conching is the term used for heating and turning the soft chocolate mixture into a perfectly blended smooth paste before being subjected to cooking and molding. This is done for hours on end by large machines containing many bearings. A breakdown in one of these machines is enormously expensive.)

The company also monitors the pumps of a regional water company, the grinding machines of a leading tool manufacturer, the turbines, generators, pumps, conveyors, and all ancillary equipment of several power stations. It serves a door manufacturing company and a health care specialist that makes artificial hips.

The width of activity now embraces the servicing of windlasses, derricks, hydraulics, pumps, gears, compressors, and generators of ocean-going bulk carriers. This is leading to a similar contract with passenger and vehicle ferry operators to monitor the main engines as well as all the other work carried out on bulk carriers.

Their present clientele, spread over a variety of industries, provides greater security for the company than its former reliance on coal.

The company has been awarded ISO 9002, the top quality certification. The business employs five people. Four are trained technicians, including Alan Smith and his son Craig. His wife, Susan, is the company administrator. Another technician is being sought to help cope with the expanding clientele. He or she will be a graduate capable of strengthening the company's theoretical knowledge. His or her employment will be an additional overhead until trained up to the performance standard maintained by the company. This training not only embraces techniques but Alan Smith's knack of knowing where to look for trouble as part of obtaining accurate prognostic information.

The strategic philosophy of the company is: "The quality of the work dominates the growth of the business." To remain a center of excellence, the search for new and more effective techniques continues relentlessly.

The following is a quote from an Insight advertisement which sets out the principle the company seeks to attain.

We are experienced engineers in Condition Monitoring and provide the following benefits to our clientele:

- Consultancy to define the problem and develop solutions
- Specialist implementation skills
- Sample and data collection and analysis
- Diagnostic services
- Training
- Results interpretation
- Plant commissioning service

Note also that the original growth of this company stemmed from the appointment of an assistant who enabled the founder to explore the possibilities of applying his skills to other business sectors.

In this case, an ability to train staff in a client's organization was a part of the excellence package. The diagnostic services were also an essential part of the product.

IMPERIAL CARPETS: AN EXAMPLE OF THE ORGANIZATION AND MANAGEMENT OF A SMALL, GROWING FIRM

Another case example shows a company, Imperial Carpets (a fictitious name), that was less successful than hoped in making carpets (its core business) but instead built up a center of excellence in carpet fittings.

Alfred Brown, the chief executive (not his real name), surveyed the state of the organization in the light of his ideas of unity of command and realized that it made big demands on its managers. Management education had been stimulated by the special needs of experimental management systems, but many executives had difficulty in coping; they felt themselves in an ambiguous position after being accustomed to clear chains of command. Yet the approach adopted retained the best of the old system—except that an individual found himself or herself in more than one system at the same time. Other experimental forms have been less dependent on chains of command and more centered on project or work groups.

Brown found much to disturb him. When he started Imperial Carpets Ltd. ten years earlier, he had no worries either of finance or personnel—he had none of either. During a period of rapid expansion he had always managed to get by. Now, with a turnover nearing £5m ($6.75m) and 350 employees, he was in financial difficulties that he had never imagined before and was becoming increasingly convinced of the inadequacies of his staff.

The financial and organizational problems were inseparably intertwined. He had not sufficient funds to finance his expansion and his inability to negotiate long-term finance was due to the fact that his profits had never matched up to his sales. Neither his results nor his organization created the right impression with those able to provide long-term loans.

The conclusion was inescapable: staffing weaknesses had produced the problems. He knew that he should delegate more and yet he found this impossible for a number of convincing reasons. Equally, he was convinced that he had appointed the most able person he could find under the circumstances. How did this paradox arise and what could be done about it?

Brown again went through the records of his five principal managers. Trevor Harvey had been with him longest and was in charge of the largest department which was also making an expensive type of carpet for the upper end of the market. Harvey's knowledge was admirable; he had proposed many new mechanical improvements which had been installed and his section had been responsible for most of the increase in sales. It also accounted for the largest investment. However, it never seemed to become profitable, and Harvey himself caused many problems. He was totally absorbed in his technical improvements and his customer relations were poor. When he was given more independence, important matters were allowed to slide. Thus he had recently left an important letter from a large customer unanswered for three weeks until Brown received a personal complaint from the managing director of the customer company.

Edward Scholes was in charge of a less prestigious but more profitable operation, making cheap fireside rugs, largely sold through street markets, fairs, and other such outlets. Brown was constantly afraid that he would lose orders from his more select customers if they found out that he was also in this type of business. But Scholes' division, although small and with a minimum of capital equipment, was making more profits than the other four divisions put together. Scholes himself was a likeable and pleasant young man, totally inexperienced, but very energetic. He had been appointed largely because his services could be obtained cheaply; he had previously been a foreman in a competitor's factory and this cheapness seemed to be in keeping with the significance of this side of the business. Because of its low prestige, Brown had kept the capital commitment of this division to a minimum; it still gave him a lot of work because he obviously could not leave Scholes to his own devices. This division also provided most of his profits, releasing resources for a center of excellence in carpet fittings.

Bert Woodhouse was in charge of another division that made a brand of carpet widely sold for use in hotel bedrooms. He was a good technical man with many bright ideas, but this was a market that was highly competitive, in which a small firm such as Imperial Carpets had difficulty in maintaining a foothold. Hence again Brown found himself spending much time in watching the moves of the competition, a subject that did not interest Woodhouse at all. Nevertheless, Woodhouse was good at providing a personal service to a customer; this ensured continuing business, but did not ensure a profitable return, as Brown now discovered.

This ability to provide a personal service to customers was seen by Brown to be the strength of a firm of this type and size and the other two divisions had grown up from this. They were both ancillary to the carpet business, one making specialized fitting tools, and the other a new device for fixing carpets which had been invented by the manager of this division himself. Both were run by highly competent technological experts whom Brown thought himself lucky to employ.

Each of the managers was paid a bonus based on the profits of his division. This seemed a sensible idea when it was introduced, but it did not appear to have made any of the carpet divisions centers of ex-

cellence in their own right. So the ultimate result was a disappointment apart from the carpet-fixing equipment. By accident, a center of
excellence had been achieved in a business that the company was not
even in.

Never forget the thought that opened this chapter:

Excellence is only excellent until a greater excellence appears.

OTHER EXAMPLES

Can Opening

Consider how often you, the reader, have had to open a can. In some
circumstances you may have used the old-fashioned solid handheld tin
opener; at other times you will have used a clip-on-and-turn-the-handle
and the whole top slides neatly off; nowadays it is possible to feed the
can into an electric machine which revolves it and neatly removes the
top. In the 1950s, Metal Box spent £250,000 ($47,000) (big money in
those far-off days) developing a revolving can opener called the Top
Hat which took the top off the can with more ease than ever before. It
was one of the earlier models of that kind. Since then and in particular
through the 1980s and early 1990s, many manufacturers, including Le-
vine and Brabantia, have come up with similar devices. The fact is that
the apparently simple task of taking the top off a tin can has caused
these manufacturers to try to create centers of excellence in edge geometry combined with food hygiene and the application of easily
cleanable plastics and stainless metals. The customer of today wants a
can opener that is permanently reliable, easy to operate, lifts the lid
neatly off the can and, at the same time, turns inward all the dangerous
jagged edges of cut tin. They are demanding excellence and there are
enough customers in the world to warrant the expense and expertise
needed to supply it.

Greenhouse Heaters

Metal Box is a center of excellence in canning technology; now
turn to consider a fictitious manufacturer of electric domestic greenhouse heaters which finds the business declining rapidly because it is
only possible to sell the product at a cutthroat price.

The management team is called together and told "The company can no longer continue to trade in this price war; we need to come up with a new product which will give outstanding performance and good value for money." After several hours of brainstorming, the company decided to design a greenhouse heater with the features listed in the box "Criteria for Center of Excellence." In setting up this task, the company is laying the keel of a center of excellence, which should stand it in good stead, restore its sales against strong competitors, and jack up its profits.

Criteria for Center of Excellence (Minimum for Greenhouse)

1. Double insulation for safety
2. A greatly reduced consumption of power
3. Complete proof against excessive damage or flooding inside the greenhouse
4. Even convection when placed centrally in the greenhouse
5. Self-operating time switches, combined with
6. Thermostatic controls
7. A built-in water reservoir with automatic humidity control
8. A built-in malfunction alarm
9. An attractive appearance
10. A reasonable warranty combined with optional service contracts
11. Excellent value for the price
12. An easy-payment finance facility

High-Tech Fasteners

Take another example of a fictitious company (Solfast Ltd.) making rivets and other kinds of fasteners for the aircraft and motor car businesses. It has received serious inquiries from the space travel and satellite industries to supply fasteners which will stand excessively high temperatures and have the flexibility to remain stable while rapidly changing to extreme cold. Here was a group of potential customers who would pay high prices for high performance products, but the company had no expertise in extreme temperature technology. It needed a center of excellence in this field. The company planned and made a search for a small business with this expertise. It eventually found High Vac Insulations (another fictitious name) which specialized in components that could stand enormous thermal shocks. This company was new, still small, reasonably profitable, but in need of additional capital for development. Solfast arranged to acquire 51 percent of the capital of High Vac Insulations at a price that would provide the necessary development finance on condition that Solfast's problems were solved in such a way as to enable it to supply the space industries.

Bridgeport Machine Tool Company

The next example of a center of excellence is the world-renowned United States-based Bridgeport Machine Tool Company—a real company! The heart of a machine tool is the driving head. Bridgeport needed thousands of perfectly functioning heads to place into machine tools being made in several factories throughout the world. To have each factory set up to make its own heads would have involved losing an economy of scale and running the risk of variance in quality. As a result, Bridgeport established a center of excellence in Singapore, which not only made heads for the company's entire output worldwide but ensured that added benefits, in particular compatibility with existing computer-driven machines, were also given to worldwide improvement. The choice of Singapore is a reminder that location also matters. The ability to manufacture high quality components at a reasonable price existed in that country.

Another Example

A company making specialized cooking equipment for Chinese restaurants was losing money because it was mishandling the difficult task of making and fitting control components. Eventually it contracted with an outside firm with the appropriate expertise to make these vital sub-assemblies. The company recovered profitability almost overnight. It had, in fact, stumbled upon a center of excellence by accident.

ISSUES OF EXCELLENCE

Consider this saying:

> Life's like a play; it is not the length but the excellence of the acting that matters.

It is the excellence that matters. Centers of excellence, such as those mentioned, are often born out of a sustained effort to beat the competition, but more than that is needed to attain universal recognition. And what?

- Ability to service long-term finance in the competitive jungle (inadequately financed companies need not apply)
- The recruitment, training, and retaining of inspired staff (companies with high staff turnover need not apply)
- Good relations with suppliers to ensure that substandard components are not received (suppliers stimulating serious complaints need not apply)
- An ability to find a location where price and quality requirements can be met (find a place with excellent physical facilities inhabited by educated and skilled people with a high morale)

Some of these issues are considered later in Part III.

Excellence, to put it differently, is an attitude rather than a set of physical facts and the attitude is that of other people; if you want to be sure that all the hard work has paid off and your company is now regarded as a center of excellence, commission an outside firm of market researchers to find out for you. Never forget to accept their verdict, even if you do not think it fair.

So how do you judge a commercial operation to be a center of excellence in spite of what has just been said? This chapter includes a number of examples of companies which had achieved centers of excellence in their industry sectors. Most of these turn out to be spin-offs from companies or individuals which had set out to crack problems found in their industries. The implications are identified in the executive summary.

Of the companies used as examples in this chapter, an existing firm (Insight Monitoring) set out to establish a center of excellence as a major article in its policy. Another, an unnamed company (Imperial Carpets), reached a center of excellence in a business ancillary to its original product; another unnamed company is seeking a reputation as a center of excellence. Yet another unnamed company (Greenhouse Heaters) has achieved a center of excellence in an especially difficult industry sector. Briefly mentioned is Metal Box, a firm that has achieved a center of excellence through years of trying; while a company that has also achieved this reputation after years of trying is Bridgeport Machine Tool. Finally, an anonymous company is another example of one that achieved a reputation for a center of excellence by accident. All of these companies are British, except Bridgeport.

These considerations do not cover the whole of the complex package that makes up a center of excellence. Other factors are considered in the following chapters but, in the end, the summary must include the word "reputation" or "recognition."

A center of excellence needs to be a firm of which outsiders will say is "well managed" or all, inside and out, will recognize that forces are at work or achievements have occurred that merit recognition above the ordinary. Excellence does not have measurable parameters; it does create an overwhelming impression. Nevertheless we will attempt a checklist to aid the recognition.

Any list of items learned in this chapter should include the long hours of work undertaken by the founder-entrepreneur and his constant dissatisfaction with results achieved so far. Insight Monitoring was an example of a company which set out purposefully to establish itself as a center of excellence.

Imperial Carpets was an example of a company, which after mediocre performance in most of its operations, achieved a center of excellence in a related but dissimilar product by accident.

Bridgeport Machine Tool achieved its reputation as a center of excellence through years of distinguished production—the most typical example of such a reputation.

A final example of an unnamed company in cooking equipment is included as another instance of arriving at a center of excellence by accident.

Consider the various examples that have been put forward and how they may be adapted for use in your business. If it is small or medium-sized (an SME!), then how can you sell a service to a company which you are already targeting as a market?

Stanley Works is a company whose product policies, outlined in the next section, illustrate this theme.

DEVELOPING TOOLS
FOR THE TWENTY-FIRST CENTURY

A continuous and successful innovator since its founding in 1843 has been the manufacturer of tools, Stanley Works, based in New Britain, Connecticut.

The Industrial Design Laboratory

Today, innovative ideas are transformed into successful new products in the industrial design laboratory which is part of the corporation's engineering and technology group. It is headed by the corporate director of industrial design who leads a team of seven highly experienced designers from a variety of industries with over 125 years of design practice among them.

Within the industrial design laboratory there is an Ergonomic Testing Laboratory. In this context, ergonomics is the art of designing the tool to obtain maximum performance efficiency with minimum human effort in optimum comfort with complete safety. The ergonomic aspect of every item is studied and checked at each stage of development.

New designs are tested by Stanley Discovery Teams drawn from the product research branch of the engineering and technical group. These people carry out field tests on new designs by working with construction professionals on building sites. Their job is to make the professionals' tasks easier and safer at the place of work. Ergonomics is the key to the process, the goal being to design tools as extensions of the human body, rather than making tools to which it has to adapt.

Project Teams

The industrial design laboratory works with the corporation's eight product groups both to conceive new ideas and to create improvements to existing products. Project teams led by the product manager—including a designer, product engineers, and marketing people—are responsible for taking the new products from conceptual stage to launch into the market. Currently the laboratory is processing forty-six projects simultaneously.

Brainstorming

The new product development process often begins with a formal brainstorming session. One or two all-day sessions are scheduled every month for the conception and consideration of new ideas. The philosophy is to identify defined and unspecified problems with a tool and then to solve them.

Challenging the conventional way of doing things is a systematic yet creative approach to problem solving.

Sketches

Designers draw sketches of ideas conceived from brainstorming sessions. These are transformed into computer models so that further modification can be made to the design.

Prototypes

Prototypes are then manufactured for performance testing in the field by the discovery team and handed to the ergonomic laboratory for human factor assessment.

The use of computer-aided design followed by the rapid making of prototypes can enable designing and testing to be carried out the same day. This, in turn, allows the project team to get complex products onto the market faster.

The FatMax Tape Rule

A good example of the development function of the industrial design laboratory is the FatMax tape rule. Working with the product manager of tape rules, the laboratory team conceived an improved tape rule with longer "standout." This involves continuously straight blade extension without its flapping downward when pulled out from the case.

The company began with a brainstorming session asking the question: "What are the major features that professionals want from a tape rule?" The discussion kept coming back to "standout." The team made a list of the possible ways that "standout" could be achieved. These ways included increased width of the tape blade, the addition of more steel into the tape, and modification of its curve.

Prototypes were produced and tested by discovery teams with professionals on building sites. They made sure that first the broader tape, and second the shape of the case and the rubber grip, would be accepted.

The result is a twenty-five and thirty-foot tape that has a "standout" of eleven feet which is acceptable to industry. It has a unique 1¼-inch wide blade with a hook, which can engage on edges above and below its tip. Though containing more steel than other types, it is lightweight and easy to hold.

Research into Grips

Among many activities in product design the textures of grips are receiving particular attention as injection molding manufacture techniques become more refined. Rugged plastics and soft rubber can be used together to create comfortable yet strong grips. The engineering design laboratory is looking at more sophisticated techniques for grips that minimize stress points and do not have sharp edges.

In the automobile world there are different types of tires for a variety of vehicles and road conditions. Likewise, grips must be compatible with the function of the tool. For example, the composition of the grip for the Stanley Multi-Bit screwdriver is totally different from that of the MaxGrip pliers, because tools are put to use by different manual actions.

The New Era of Tool Design

Stanley Works is in a new era of tool design and development. It is challenging the basic laws of physics and questioning everything that can be seen from the products described in the following text, and it is a leader in tool design and innovation.

The Stanley IntelliTape digital tape rule is a full-function electronic tape rule that gives traditional and digital measurements in both imperial and metric graduations. It has a heavy duty one-inch lacquered steel blade, an easy-to-read digital display memory storage, freeze display, and a midpoint memory function. It has a zero reset facility enabling calculation of distance between several points.

The Stanley IntelliMeasure Laser Estimator is a hand-held device which quickly calculates the square footage and volume of rooms, floors, and walls. It can handle distances up to fifty feet and measurements are shown on an easy-to-read digital display in both imperial and metric graduations.

The Stanley IntelliSensor Digiscan Stud Sensor is a high-powered stud sensor which detects and differentiates wood, metal, and live wires simultaneously through a variety of wall thicknesses and materials. The user can calibrate the tool to the wall within one or two seconds. A liquid crystal display with easy-to-read icons shows the type of material detected. Its powerful deep scan function detects live wires at both three- and four-inch depths, and metal at three inches of wall thickness.

Innovation at Stanley Works raises some interesting points for readers to consider:

- Is our research and development department structured for our present and future innovative aspirations?
- Are our research and development people adequately qualified and experienced for the innovation tasks ahead?
- Do we "brainstorm" our innovation challenges?
- Do we ever challenge conventional ways of function, traditional styles, and long-accepted standards?
- Do we make use of competent project teams?
- Are our product-testing procedures sufficiently realistic and thorough for ensuring user or consumer acceptance?

CENTERS OF EXCELLENCE: A CHECKLIST

- The vital targets
- Staffing—the recruitment and training of innovators
- In-house or contracting out?
- Design
- Research
- Hi-tech

All of these are elaborated in the following chapters.

Chapter 8

Staffing: The Innovative Atmosphere

The success of everything proposed in this book depends on the individual, the personality. How are these innovative, enterprising characters to be identified to fill the key strategic positions in a company? The answer lies in three words: recruitment, training, motivation. This chapter explains how the activities summed up by these words operate in the real world. However, keep in mind that the best laid schemes frequently fail. The best insurance against failure is for the recruit to come into an atmosphere at work that encourages and promotes the objectives for which he or she has been recruited—in this case, the innovative atmosphere.

PREPARING THE COMPANY

The first question to answer is: how can the usefulness of the existing staff be improved? This means a process of frank appraisal of existing staff and their potential. This is not a book about personnel management, so this subject is not explored in detail. Before undertaking any search, the possibility of training an existing member of staff in the most advanced thinking about personnel and training management (human resources, if you will) needs to be decided; in a small or middle-sized company the two jobs (personnel and training) are likely to be combined in one person. This may not be an ideal arrangement, but staff costs must be kept down. When the number of employees exceeds 4,000 (to pick a figure out of the air) training becomes a full-time department with the training manager reporting to the personnel manager. If either post cannot be filled by an existing employee, recruitment from outside becomes necessary and will be considered next. Recruitment from outside can demoralize an organization unless the reasons for it are very obvious. Similarly, promotion from inside boosts the morale as long as it is considered to be justified; no one is impressed by the promotion of ineffective employees due to seniority or other irrelevant reasons.

After agreeing that recruitment from outside is a last resort, the critical consideration is that it only takes place when internal promotion is genuinely proved to be impossible. The usual argument for recruitment from outside is that the new employee will bring fresh ideas and a different outlook to those inside. That may be a problem, as the new member of staff has not lived through the process of developing a center of excellence and is unlikely to understand the factors that have conditioned the outlooks, the reactions, and the ambitions of those inside. The difficulty of inside recruiting is that every possible candidate will have a battery of enemies who may prove uncooperative; the recruit will soon collect friends to give support, and some enemies, too, who may prove troublesome. As suggested elsewhere in this book, some difficult interpersonal relationships leading to friction do not necessarily harm the organization.

Friction, let us repeat, can be creative. All the same, strong leadership is required to prevent a company from descending into a morass of warring factors. Force a recruit (whether internal or external) to carry out the task with sights firmly focused on new product development.

One of the present authors had experience of the difficulties of internal recruitment when he made arrangements for an employee to receive computer training when the company needed a computer specialist. The training came to an end when he was told that there was no hope that she, the employee in question, would ever be able to cope.

RECRUITMENT

Is the company ready for the recruitment? Most executives would ask that question first. And how do you tell? Those of us who have grown old in the service of business or in the writing of books (and that means most of us over thirty) easily forget how much a youthful, go-getting atmosphere in which new ideas are encouraged and not frowned upon, means to young recruits. They do not need to be put in positions where every suggestion is shot down in flames and the dread (senile) words "we've tried that and it didn't work" spring to their manager's lips. Perhaps it didn't work but that's no excuse for not trying it again, even if only to encourage the new recruit.

The processes of selection and recruitment are complicated. Some will prefer to use consultants. There is little evidence that this method produces more or less satisfactory results than direct advertisement and interview but, if an outside consultant is to be employed, a carefully compiled and scrutinized briefing is needed. Too often the briefing goes unprepared. When it is drafted it is likely to be finalized by the project team with which the new recruit will be working. The reason for this is that innovation is not likely to be a full-time appointment so the briefing must be well-integrated with the mainstream activity which the recruit is to undertake.

Outside recruitment advisers have much to be said for them, especially when new ideas are sought in the recruit, but there is one major snag: the recruitment consultant usually forms a picture of who the company really wants and this picture may be heavily biased as a result of experience in other firms and thus not fit this client. Consultants tend to go for smooth-talking people who have chalked up a number of successes at an early age. The very successes may have closed their minds; beware of people who boast about their "experience." The only "experience" required is of managing innovative product lines; the candidate may be less articulate on this subject and the consultant may go for articulateness rather than genuine understanding and depth of innovative motivation.

The same may be true if the company is recruiting directly. The whole job needs to be outlined in the advertisement and during the interview. At this time the candidates will be given a relevant role-play followed by a set of targets, mainly aimed at their innovating role and membership of a project group. The person appointed will be served with a list of targets, not necessarily a job description—that relic of obsolete so-called "scientific management" some would call it. A set of targets for each activity is needed; their attainments (or approach) will be a condition of employment. A modern approach is made with job specifications that are target or goal oriented. This approach safeguards the bias toward innovation needed in the staffing function. The person appointed will be directed toward innovation but she or he will have to do some mainstream or routine work as well.

The ideal method of recruitment would be to take on a person for a temporary period, say a month, so that he or she can see and be seen.

The firm's ability to do this will depend on its reputation and the state of the national economy at the time. When jobs are scarce, recruits can be found this way; when the economy is booming, it is likely to be impossible. In either case, let us agree that a willingness to take on a temporary assignment may itself be evidence of the kind of character required. However, no one is likely to accept a temporary job even with a most attractive company when faced with a firm permanent offer from a company which does not appear to the candidate to be that much worse.

Be realistic: try on the temporary offer ploy. The kind of character required may be so self-confident that the offer will not be regarded as temporary. In any event, a candidate may appear ideal and so the temporary offer may be considered irrelevant, which leads to the further comment that articulate candidates may not be the most suitable. Hire a professional psychologist able to look into character at some depth, so long as it is remembered that the advice given is just that: advice.

In regard to selection consultants and psychologists, listen to their advice and follow your own judgment. Above all, know whom the company needs; age, gender, and race are all irrelevant beside personal qualities and track record. Never forget to check on references and to confirm the truth of the track record.

Most important, as has been said already, is the atmosphere into which the newcomer is being recruited. If it is negative, and every proposal for innovation is automatically turned down, the recruit will adapt all too quickly to proposing only well-worn paths that will be assumed to be more acceptable. The innovative atmosphere is crucial to recruitment. Newcomers must feel from the start that their performance will be judged by the new ideas they bring, even if an occasional expensive failure is included. Of course, expensive failures cannot be tolerated too often.

APPOINTMENT

The innovative firm is one in which the likings of old-fashioned bureaucrats are not honored. Out must go old-style job specifications and anything else which exalts minimum performance. The recruit has been appointed to an innovative company and not one in which the adherence to rules, organization charts, and other bureaucratic paraphernalia take the recruit's attention away from the main purpose of fostering the firm and its products. Assuming the recruit is a non-technical person, it will be necessary to get to know the technical people as soon as possible. A regular lunch meeting with technical staff is a useful arrangement.

This may cause long-time employees to opt out of a card school or keep fit class once in a while. However, recruits must have a higher authority to whom they can appeal in spite of the dislike of bureaucracy detailed earlier in this chapter—a dislike which must be modified to suit circumstances. Someone must be in charge in a business organization, but that does not mean that procedures and organization charts will be allowed to cramp the corporate style. The recruit from outside is likely to need an ally (call that person a mentor if you will) to establish working relationships with the veterans among the new colleagues.

The problem of the veteran employee who pours cold water on the enthusiasm of the newcomer must not be overlooked. Persistent obstructors must be told that there is no longer a place for them in the company, however long their service.

TRAINING

The discussion in this chapter points to the need for training, a training which is likely to be as formal as the approach of the firm to other issues is informal. However "informal," it will need to be organized and to be ongoing. Business training is much in the news these days, but training for the innovative company means opening the eyes of participants to new ideas and where to find them.

Then why do we need a training program? The answer is, it is not simple for most people who find the demands of training in conflict with other demands the company makes upon them. Instruction in formal procedures is only needed by technical staff, others need guidance about working with technical staff and turning their activities into profit. One well-known engineering company announced in 1997 that executive directors must go through twenty-five days of training courses every year, and that figure is a minimum for all employees, including lengthy training programs for the most junior.

The demands of the innovative atmosphere require that existing managers control themselves when they want to ridicule the new recruit's efforts and suggestions. Of course, damage must be limited, but talents do not need to be suppressed.

IDEAS PEOPLE

"Mr X, all our futures depend upon a steady stream of new ideas. They must be commercial, and if they are good ideas together we can turn them into profitable ones. If not, we are all out of a job even faster than if we never had the ideas."

This kind of atmosphere takes years to build up and can easily be destroyed by one arrogant employee, a mistake in the recruitment process. Employees cannot be forced to work harmoniously together. Very few do, and friction within a firm as well as in a family can turn out to be a constructive force.

Out of friction—strong disagreements, for example—can come solutions that would never have been reached if the company was too harmonious. Aneurin Bevan, the founder of the National Health Service in Britain, is often considered an outstanding cabinet minister and himself no mean provoker of friction as his colleagues came to know only too well. He once said that an organization within which everyone gets on well with everyone else is dead. Peace, perfect peace, is the most obvious symptom of a corpse. We are not looking for corpses but for active, vibrant organizations in which all the participants stand up for themselves, prepared to fight for their own turf. Of course, that means a willingness on all sides to admit to the possibility of error and to compromise in order to negotiate a final solution. Naturally, friction can also be destructive; the innovative manager needs to develop a skill in handling friction among staff.

Some of the great innovative managers of the past fifty years, such as Wilfred Brown, have shown a willingness not so much to compromise (that may not work) but at least to move the argument on to fresh ground where a constructive agreement can be achieved. That makes conflict constructive, a begetter of new possibilities, a training ground for innovators. Naturally strong leadership is needed to contain friction and to ensure that no harm is done.

STAFFING

A number of questions to ask:

- Is this company making the best use of existing staff?

The answer is: of course not, no company is. We all need to do better.

- Everyone needs to play a part in the training.

The technique that used to be called "action learning" is used by successful companies. This means that all the participants are allocated problems that need to be solved. They make use of acknowledged experts to arrive at their solutions which then have to be defended against arguments from the other members of the group.

- We have to accept that for some, no amount of training will produce results. Their work cannot be improved and they have no future with a company for which they are spending money, not earning it.
- That acceptance comes after much effort, but the timing must be limited so that no one is given the chance to say: "So and so gave x years of his or her life to the company only to be ditched when it suited them." Such statements do not boost morale.
- No company should guarantee employment for life. Retraining must be attempted but, in the end, dismissal can sometimes be the only course. This is not a subject for this book except to say that any action must appear fair. A reputation for keeping people who are making no worthwhile contribution is a sure way of sinking that treasured morale—a morale that must be retained if opportunities for new product development are to come to light.

It is no good arguing that the arbitrary dismissal of someone or sentimentally retaining someone else is an advantage to a company.

There are two extremes in staffing policies. In its heyday the British electronics firm, Plessey, an example of one extreme, would employ senior people to take charge of a new product project on a contract which lasted no longer than the time taken to get the new product out to the market, at which time the employment came to an end.

Surprisingly, talented project directors, scientists, designers, engineers, and others would come back to and leave Plessey over and over again to take part in various new product projects. It was good, in those days, to have Plessey on your resumé.

An example of the other extreme is the Acclaim Cooker Company (not its real name). Mr. P has been director of product development for fifteen years with a small staff of two designers, each with ten years' service. This small team developed rigid prejudices about design, heat distribution, function, and performance criteria. Only through enormous pressure from the chief executive, backed by the other directors, would Mr. P follow up very good ideas coming from the market, from comparison with competitive products, and from their own salespeople. The company's record in new products was pathetic and they were surviving by selling on low prices and low profit margins against competitive products which had many innovative features.

Depending on a variety of factors such as high-tech content, scientific specialism, and design dependence, most companies are staffing their innovation function somewhere between these two extremes.

A director or manager in charge of the product development function has a line relationship with the staff of the department. But he or she is the boss whose relationship with the chairman is staff because the department is helping to create the innovation undertaken as the result of *executive* decision and action.

It stands to reason therefore that people who work full time in product development are hired because they bring a specialism or expertise which the company needs to maintain a continuous outflow of new products and services: scientists, chemists, designers, draftsmen, model makers, electronic engineers, and dieticians.

As projects become imminent, a company has to decide whether to employ people or to put the work out, and this decision will affect staffing. If, for example, a chemical problem or decision seldom arises, then it may be better to subcontract the work content of the project. If, on the contrary, dietetic problems need attention in every project, then it is better to employ a dietician permanently.

People hired for service in the research and development department usually bring their specialism and expertise with them. Their training includes two subjects: (1) learning more and more about the company's markets, products, and business characteristics; (2) self-improvement, for example: the designer will be encouraged to learn modern and progressive design techniques, while the electronics engineer will strive to keep up with progress in electronic technology.

A firm has to be ready to lose members of the research and development teams if they keep on improving their knowledge and capability and the company fails to feed them tasks which tax their improved performance standards or provide money to pay for their expertise.

Contracts: Retaining the Staff

Your company will not wish to lose staff who have been won through such an exacting process of recruitment and induction. One essential for this purpose is a contract giving terms and conditions for severance; without this, an employee can walk out on very short notice and take part of your business. A booklet titled *Contract of Employment* (Institute of Personnel and Development, 1999) explains the need for a contract and the present state of employment law which shows the detail required in the contract (for the address of the IPD, see the end of the chapter).

CONCLUSION

- Staffing for innovation depends on an innovative atmosphere throughout the company.
- Start with existing staff when possible.
- No money spent on training is wasted as long as the objectives are closely followed.
- Recruitment from outside requires a vibrant go-getting atmosphere that can absorb and inspire the recruit.
- Briefing for recruits closely follows innovation alongside the mainstream activity.
- Hire for a fixed term if practicable.
- Listen to psychologists and consultants but always follow your own judgment.
- Strong disagreements must be contained but, on principle, friction can be creative.

- Issues that come up regularly require the hiring of a specialist expert on the issue.
- Have an adequate consumer test panel.

G. R. WRIGHT AND SONS

Innovation: A Family Tradition

"Tradition," said King Faisal of Saudi Arabia, "should be made the ally of development. The surest progress comes through tradition, for, though it might make change slower, it also makes it surer" (Lacey, 1981, p. 368).

G. R. Wright and Sons have been milling flour at Ponders End Mill on the banks of the River Lea at Enfield near London, England, since 1867. The site had been occupied by various flour mills driven by waterwheel since 1067.

Quality

George Reynolds Wright, the first chairman, established the principle: products bearing his name would be made only of the finest ingredients using the most modern techniques. This criterion is still applied four generations later by his great great grandson, David Wright, the present managing director.

Modernization

Throughout its history there has been continuous innovation in the plant, such as installing the continental roller mill system, retaining millstones only for certain speciality products, and replacing water power by electricity. Through the first and second world wars the company had to operate under government control as did all food manufacturers and producers in the United Kingdom.

Following World War I, regulation continued until 1920. Deregulation sparked off a period of cutthroat competition on price, exacerbated by the Great Depression. Millers all over the country suffered for a decade and many had to close or sell out.

Investment During Depression

G. R. Wright and Son handled the depression years by investing heavily in a new plant to be ready to exploit the future economic recovery. For example, in 1925 it constructed a 600-ton silo, the tallest building in the district. During World War II the company was compelled to run the mill around the clock seven days a week to make up for the lost production of other mills, which had been destroyed by enemy bombing.

A Modern Mill

This enormous wear and tear created ideal conditions for yet further renewal of the plant through the postwar years. Through the 1970s the standard of packaging improved throughout the industry. Today, Ponders End Mill is a modern computer-controlled food factory complete with state-of-the-art packaging machinery capable of filling seventy-five 500-gram packs per minute and a carousel packaging machine to load the large bags. The mill has been awarded BS EN ISO 9002 accreditation, the highest international standard for quality assurance. In the 1860s, the annual output was 1,000 tons. Today that quantity is turned out in less than a week.

The company supplies flour products not only for small bakers, in-store bakeries, plant bakeries, and biscuit operations, but also to industrial customers such as starch manufacturers.

"Value" Flour

Through the 1990s, history repeated itself. The flour market in the United Kingdom became a penny bazaar. Fewer people were baking at home. To generate sales, supermarket chain stores began selling "value" flour at exceptionally low prices, which still prevails today. Large and small mills, therefore, have had to cut their margins severely to stay in the market. This is a situation in which millers, packers, and the supermarkets themselves are selling at a loss.

Top Quality Cake Mixes

G. R. Wright and Sons are climbing above this dissipating competition. They have installed a plant which, though automated, is flexible and capable of short runs of a range of a variety of products in distinctive packs.

This has enabled the company to move into the production of bread mixes. Through the efficiency of the plant these can be sold at prices attractive to the consumer, yet profitable to the company.

Bread mixes consist of a mixture of flour, yeast, and a distinctive mix of ingredients if desired. To make bread from these products, the domestic consumer need only add water, mix, shape into a loaf or several rolls, allow time for rising, and place into the oven. Use of bread mixes saves the arduous and time-consuming tasks of conventional bread making. The bread mixes are also ideally suited to domestic bread-making machines, which are in general use in Canada and the United States, and are gaining popularity in Europe.

The company's market research revealed that, as a result of overseas travel, the British are developing a taste for traditional bread from other countries.

Wright's range of bread mixes attractively presented in 500-gram packages include mixed grain, premium white, wholemeal, chili, naan (an Indian mix), malty (malt and bran), scofa (the name is derived from Scottish farl, a traditional round loaf from Scotland made without yeast), ciabatta (an Italian loaf, normally shaped like a slipper), parmesan and sun-dried tomatoes, organic and stoneground wholemeal. The company also manufactures some of these products for supermarket chains under their own label.

Keeping to the company's tradition this range of bread mixes is made from the highest quality of flour, mainly from Canadian wheat. There are twelve more mixes prepared and ready to launch on the market to meet new competition.

Competition

Competition is steadily increasing. Similar mixes are being introduced by the largest milling organization in Britain and others have launched packs of seed and grain to add to conventional bread making. This competition is sure to intensify, stimulated by the increasing demand for domestic bread-making machines in the United Kingdom.

Originally the company supplied bread mixes in bulk to commercial bakers. Introduction of the consumer range, mainly sold in supermarkets, has in no way disturbed good business relationships with primary customers.

Ethnic Communities

Following its strategy to supply special products, the company has carved out a substantial market for selling distinctive flours including premium quality Chipatti flour to bakers catering to the Asian communities in the United Kingdom. It is also exporting these products into a niche market and its bread mixes are being imported to the West Indies.

Everyone Involved in Innovation

While the managing director is involved in all innovation, the company's research and development is led by the technical director, who is also responsible for quality assurance.

Within the general plant there is a well-equipped laboratory and a test bakery. New products can be created very quickly. They are tested not only for consumer acceptance but also for practicability of manufacture.

The company is involved in the enhancement of bread improvers, replacing soya and maintaining the right balance of ascorbic acid (vitamin C).

Consumer Testing

Consumer testing panels are the company employees, their friends, and families. These comprise enough people to provide a reliable opinion sample. Each person's assessment is guided by a questionnaire.

Any bread mix demanded by a supermarket chain for its own label is tested in conjunction with the customer's staff. This is not always an easy process. On the one hand the suitability of the company's offer is based on the opinions of a large number of people. The customer's judgment, on the other hand, can be the result of a test by a small panel.

Public Relations

The company runs a home baking club, which consumers are invited to join. They receive recipes and other information including details of new products.

The main promotional thrust is by public relations activity including demonstrations at regional meetings of the Women's Institute and the Townswomen's Guild. Their products are on display at county agricultural shows all over the United Kingdom.

Export trade is increasing, including a demand from the West Indies, Holland, and Spain.

Performance

Over the past five years, the company profitability has expanded at a compound rate of 60 percent. "Wright's Mill stands as a glowing example of determination and entrepreneurship, a symbol of the ability of a family business to adapt product and processes to the needs of a highly competitive and ever-changing industrial world" (Lewis, 1999, p. 11).

G. R. Wright and Sons innovative tradition raises some interesting points that the readers might like to consider.

- What is the main tradition of our business? Does it carry us forward in our present and future dealings?
- Are we financially sound to ride out a depression without stunting our long-term growth through short-term measures?
- Are we sure we are not drawn into a low quality, low price trade situation?
- Is our manufacturing capability flexible? Or are we saddled with a fixed automated plant for mass production of a narrow range of products?
- Do we have new products held in reserve to meet new competition?
- Do we have an adequate consumer test panel?

What Have We Learned from This Chapter?

Hiring (recruitment) needs to be planned to bring required skills and attitudes into the company. The recruit must be able to guide the company to the excellence that is being sought.

It follows from the argument in the latter part of the chapter that training for senior managers must be individual, related to the role that they will be expected to perform in a company. This may seem wasteful, and it certainly raises problems about who is to conduct the training. Perhaps a senior manager or one with specific training duties who calls on other managers from inside the firm as well as outside experts can undertake training sessions. The example of Wright's flour demonstrates that tradition can sometimes be useful.

Useful Address

The Institute of Personnel and Development, 35 Camp Road, London.

Chapter 9

In-House or Contracting Out?

This ancient conundrum still has to be answered with contemporary relevance, that is, answered pragmatically, practically. The question has a special relevance to new product development: it may be impossible to bring a new product to market quickly enough without subcontracting.

"Anything we can do ourselves, we do." That is one doctrine you will have heard. The opposite states: "We concentrate only on things we can do well. The rest we subcontract." Both these views are attractive. The first, the achievement of excellence with one product or service, leads to the conviction that a center of excellence in one product can be achieved in others. This is, of course, misleading, ignoring the complicated package of factors that together make up a center of excellence. Totally different skills are required by a publisher of magazines from those required by a book publisher although both are called "publishers." Admittedly, success in either case rests on a close understanding of target readers, but under what circumstances is closeness to the market not needed for success? Contracting out is needed when speed to market is essential either with a view to keeping up with competitors or leap-frogging ahead of them.

The other view, that offers anything that can be subcontracted to the best bidder is also unsatisfactory; it may rob a firm of useful outlets for its staff. Why hire and train so conscientiously and then ignore the results by subcontracting to outside businesses?

If view one is "do not subcontract" and view two is "subcontract wherever possible," the compromise proposed here does not lie at some central point between the two, it leans heavily toward the second view—subcontract where possible without ignoring home-grown talent.

And why?

The answer lies in a common feature of the search for excellence. That is the experience that redundant skills or knowledge will be produced along the way. If these cannot be exploited commercially, they should be. Obviously.

Suppose, for instance, your company produced a revolutionary new style of food freezer cabinet. It kept the food at a predetermined temperature without the necessity for defrosting and other fuel-wasting attention. It was also of larger capacity but lighter in weight than existing models so that it could be moved easily when the house was being reorganized, demanding specifications which would also command wide sales and allow a satisfactory margin.

So what may have happened in the development of this project? The company may well have increased its knowledge of freezer technology and be well on the way to establishing a global reputation for excellence in this technology. Its main thrust will probably have been toward this reputation which will be profitable in a number of ways. For instance, it is likely to have enlarged the market by lowering the price of the product, but the company will be well aware that the research that led to the improvements was not a unique technology. On the contrary, its competitors shared much of the basic knowledge and would be all too likely to be first in the market with a highly saleable product. This made speed essential and proved a dilemma for the company which was to identify which components of the electrical system were part of the breakthrough and which were already in use. The latter—electrical components already in use—could be delegated to an outside contractor to enable the new freezer to be marketed more quickly. The company had not invented, or patented, the devices linking the new freezer to the electrical supply system and these can most profitably be subcontracted; *unless* the company has produced new techniques along the way which will go to make additions to the center of excellence, in this case established subcontracts will be canceled.

Normally the view that resources should be ditched because of a doctrinaire attachment toward concentrating on the core business only means that the excellence has not penetrated the top decision making in the firm. A company that has made itself a special reputation in one branch of chemical production may well find another. This will not be a spreading and diluting of its excellence, although the money markets—where dilution is unpopular—may think it means just that. Rest assured that any reduction in the share price will soon be replaced by an increase when the success of this particular move becomes apparent.

This bias toward diversification and toward the encouragement of skills and expertise which deviate from a company's main route is harmless, *so long as* no resources are moved into the deviation which are needed by the core activity. In most firms this will be watched for, but it cannot be watched too carefully. In fact, this issue is mainly of interest to manufacturers; most service operators will not suffer from it. They will probably possess a variety of expertise which will in no way influence the main thrust. Crucial to the argument is that the main thrust must be maintained with top priority if the excellence is to be preserved.

Let us consider three companies which have reacted in different ways to problems on the route, all three are anonymous but described from the authors' knowledge; since the authors stand in a relation of confidentiality, the business must be adequately disguised. These examples are followed by a named company which has gradually built up a worldwide reputation for excellence.

Company A is a world famous technical consultancy. In one of its engineering products it is widely recognized as a world center of excellence. In the process of acquiring the recognition, company A added relevant management requirements to its technical skills. Arguably it was this addition that turned an inspired activity into a center of excellence. A case has been promoted suggesting that the company could acquire the same reputation for a similar product. Most of the board members were convinced. They had the resources, the directors argued, and their existing reputation would add credibility to the project.

Strong arguments, but the chief executive was adamant.

"We decided long ago not to dilute our efforts," he banged the table. "If we accept this proposal, it will be followed by others equally plausible. And where will it all end?

"Our staff are already turning into fat cats on the strength of what we are doing now. Beware a move that might destroy our profitability."

THE COMPANY B STRATEGY

The second unnamed company (B) is one in which the board is unanimously of the opinion that the product base is too narrow. The directors know full well that they have generated resources which are currently underemployed. Company B went to the opposite extreme from company A. Everything must be done in-house. The snags to this approach soon became obvious and the company modified its policy to avoid being swamped with new employees to meet the timing of the new product strategy. In the future, a development department was to be set up as new products loomed on the company horizon. Talented employees who were surplus to requirements were to be drafted into the new departments and encouraged to undergo a period of retraining to match their new responsibilities.

This company B strategy should meet the needs of most firms, although it will also be adapted in many ways to suit individual circumstances. It amounts to: "Let us concentrate on our core strategy while watching out for surplus resources—knowledge, skills, funds—that can be put to profitable use."

In any case the new product strategy follows after the main corporate strategy has been worked out. First, we know where we are going; second, we must work out targets for new products along the way which will improve the company's profits and ensure the corresponding strategy is kept on course. Given this, the tactical issue of whether the elements are contracted out will solve itself. This, like most statements in this book, applies to manufacturing and service industries equally. The successful entrepreneur in retailing, transport, or law notes how much knowledge and skill the existing staff have acquired in the slow race to a reputation for excellence; a realistic calculation can then be made on the subject of retraining and reorientation.

An ancient and boring saying goes something like this: "Build a better mousetrap and the world will beat a path to your door." Nothing is said about what the RSPCA (animal protection people) will be doing in the meantime. This book is about a more subtle means of persuading the world to beat a path to your door—by a painfully slow process of building up a reputation. This uses to the full design expertise, sympathy for the customer and public relations and promotional techniques that among them gradually convince a skeptical world that you have the solution to an age-old worry—where to turn for a certain product or service that people cannot help but need. The reputation is better sustained if the "world" is convinced that the excellence is supported by a command of the ancillary products or services.

A third company (C), reported from an assignment undertaken by one of the present authors, made cookers for Chinese restaurants. Although company C dominated the market for equipment for Chinese restaurants in Britain, the company was experiencing severe losses. When the supply of one vital ingredient was subcontracted, the company moved into profit.

One company that has provided an example of product innovation for this chapter (Carbolite of Hope Valley near Sheffield, England) is at the leading edge of specialist furnace production; most products are tailored to individual customers and so are all innovations of which examples are given in the text. Under the circumstances it is clear that each product has to be manufactured in a hurry.

A COMPANY LED BY INNOVATION

Carbolite, founded in 1938, is the largest manufacturer of laboratory furnaces and ovens in the United Kingdom. Its range of models used in both research and production embraces many applications. These include: sterilization, incubation, drying, heat treatment, melting, calibration, ashing, analysis, firing, and crystal growing.

Carbolite furnaces vary in size from that of a small lap top computer to that of a huge treble garage. Further, the company can produce gas-cooled chambers at −150°C at one extreme and +2,000°C at the other.

Up to 600°C, the products are called ovens; above that temperature they are usually known as furnaces. The company's clients are from many industries including aerospace, automobiles, ceramics, glass, iron and steel, mining, pharmaceuticals, chemicals, engineering, electronics, plastics, and other composites. Products are exported to more than 100 countries.

An Ever-Increasing Range of Products

The company produces a full standard range of simple laboratory furnaces in which the heat distribution is electronically controlled, providing a performance read out. Specially designed doors protect the operator from a blast of heat when they are opened. The major activity of the business, however, is the manufacture of "specials" to handle customers' particular problems in the area of heat application. Here are a few examples.

The Carbolite Asphalt Binder Analyzer is a redesigned version of a United States invention. It is used when it is essential to highway construction to maintain continuous control of the mixture of asphalt and bitumen. Traditionally this has been achieved by using solvents. This method, which involves chlorinated chemicals, causes health and environmental hazards and is being made obsolete by switching to furnaces. A sample of mixture is placed in the analyzer furnace which burns off the bitumen and at the same time records the consequent weight loss, thus producing an accurate reading of the original mix. The smoke arising from the operation is burned out in a secondary furnace, thus eliminating any environmental concern. Today this type of analyzer is made by Carbolite in Britain and by two manufacturers in the United States and it is marketed successfully in the United Kingdom, the United States, the Middle East, and Southeast Asia.

Another product is for the aerospace industry. A French manufacturer of industrial fasteners was making bolts for a major United States aircraft company. To harden them, bolts were being heated in bulk in a furnace to 1,300°C before being quenched. The degree of hardness was not satisfactory and it was necessary to raise the temperature to 1,350°C. At this point the bolts began to melt and fuse into each other. To overcome this problem, Carbolite devised a mechanical tube-shaped furnace containing a special "helter skelter" type carriage to convey the bolts, each in a separate compartment, through the furnace and out into a quench (a pool of water or other liquid). This form of furnace is now being developed also for laboratory applications.

Yet another product is to fuse a protective coating on to Turbine blades. This involved an extension of the so-called "top hat" type of furnace. This furnace was developed to enable heavy bulk or voluminous quantities of small items to be placed inside without lifting gear. The objects to be heated are placed on a flat hearth and the furnace (shaped like a deep box lid) is lowered over the hearth encasing it before the heat is applied. To obtain a satisfactory fusion of coating on turbine blades, four different furnace applications were required. This was achieved by placing four hearths in line and designing mechanisms to lower the "top hat" furnace onto each one in turn.

In addition to these products the company turns out rotary and mesh belt furnaces for continuous sintering (heat treating certain metals—iron, tin, nickel, copper, and aluminium among them)—to a temperature just below their melting point and furnaces for the continuous heat treatment of wire and metal strip. The latter includes the fine gauge wires used to probe human arteries.

Recently the company has designed an annealing furnace capable of maintaining low levels of contamination and oxidization while heat treating electric relay components and cores for electric motor windings. These components require magnetic annealing to enhance their performance after pressing while maintaining a completely bright finish. To meet the requirements, the components are processed in a pure hydrogen atmosphere. In normal use the furnace takes loads weighing 100 to 200 kilograms and holds them at temperatures up to 1,150°C for twenty-four hours.

Carbolite did not add industrial ovens to its product range until it took over an established oven manufacturer in Eastern England in the early 1980s. The demand for ovens is now overtaking that for furnaces. This reflects the worldwide increase in pharmaceutical and medical research activity. Ovens are used for growing cells and bacteria as well as other analyzing processes.

This upsurge of research activity is now creating an even stronger market for incubators than for ovens. As a result, the company is being drawn into the design and manufacture of incubators.

It now produces a "Paternoster" style incubator, which is used in the mass screening of drugs and forms part of a fully automated style laboratory. The incubator chamber contains a rotating mechanism which indexes a series of horizontal trays. In front of the incubator there is a "posting slot" to allow a robot to place plates of samples in the "paternoster" tray.

Designers Are Crucial

Out of a total complement of 120 people, nineteen are employed in design, four of them work continuously on product improvement, the remainder on innovation. The latter are usually the heads of project groups. Designers are equipped with up-to-date CAD (computer aided design) hardware and software. The shape and positioning of rivet holes on a furnace panel can be relayed directly to a panel cutting and drilling machine on the factory floor from a CAD computer in the design department.

Substantial improvement in product performance as well as cost reduction has been achieved by close liaison and consultation between designers and shop floor operators. For example, such cooperation has led to the production of an efficient low-cost oven, through a 30 percent reduction of manufacturing costs of which 15 percent has been passed onto the customer.

Open House Laboratory

Hand in glove with design, the company has a well-equipped laboratory for experimentation in all aspects of furnace technology including heat control. The laboratory is operated on an open-house basis, no one has overall control, it is open for use by any employee or group of employees engaged in research and development projects.

Testing Integrated with Factory Flowline

There is also a specialist department for calibrating (arranging measurements for) and programing electronic heat controls, read outs, and print outs before these are installed into furnaces and ovens.

The final testing of appliances before they enter the despatch department, known as "burning off," is carried out in a specialized testing section.

These topics of experimentation and testing are dovetailed into the factory flowline system. The flowline comprises panel making, fabrication, painting, the fitting of elements, refractories and insulation, assembly of moving parts, and the final assembly of electronic controls and testing. An interesting feature of the factory is the vacuum forming of ceramic fiber insulation to any desired shape with or without the elements integrated into it.

In-House or Buy In

The company is quality accredited to ISO 9001 (a high-level international standard) and makes everything in-house except elements, insulation, and electronic controls which are bought in from specialist manufacturers.

Currently deep consideration is being given to two factors concerning supplies of electronic controls. First by relying on bought-in subassemblies, flexibility is restricted. Second, outside suppliers could develop new and improved apparatus for Carbolite, and with slight modifications make the new techniques available to competitors. The practicability of redeveloping an electronic capability in-house is being studied.

Value for Money

Today the company is recognized worldwide as a center of excellence in the field of distribution and control of heat. Nevertheless, it operates in the face of tough competition, especially from Germany.

Some three years ago, the differentiation of currency value between the strong pound sterling and the weak deutsche mark was creating a 40 percent price advantage to German equipment. This problem has now been overcome by continuous design improvement and value engineering to produce products which measure up to performance standard at competitive prices with adequate profit margins to the company. The strength of the pound sterling is no longer an obstacle to expanding sales at home and abroad.

Hands-On Research and Development Management

The company employs a research and development manager with direct responsibility to the production director for ensuring innovative projects are carried out to quality standard within budget and on time. The product development committee is chaired by the managing director. It includes the production and marketing directors and the research and development manager and screens ideas and monitors progress on all innovations including new customer specials.

Under this close governance of its innovative effort, Carbolite is able to maintain its lead over competitors through the performance of its products, most of which are created by special requirements of customers to overcome particular problems.

This is why, in addition to maintaining its establishment as a center of excellence, it employs a large staff of well-equipped designers to create a continuous flow of successful new products. Carbolite is an innovation-oriented company.

Ovens Supplied to BPL at Elstree

During the early 1980s Carbolite worked very closely with the Central Blood Laboratories Authority to develop an oven for heat treating Factor VIII, a blood-derived product, to eliminate the viruses of hepatitis and AIDS. The process requires the product to be heated for a long time at a very accurate and stable temperature (70°C ± 1°C).

Because of the very high value of the product in the oven, £50,000 ($69,500), great consideration has gone into making the equipment reliable and incorporating safety features that will shut down the oven if a fault should occur. It is most important that the product is not subjected to any temperatures higher than the treatment temperature. If a fault occurs the forced cooling facility will ensure that the product temperature is reduced to ambient temperature as soon as possible. It is possible to re-treat the product after a fault if a record of the process is kept. The oven is fitted with two chart recorders, a main multichannel and a back-up single channel to ensure as far as possible that a record of any heat treatment process will always be available.

Following the successful development of the process, a total of six units have been supplied to the British authority. Two additional units have been supplied to the Red Cross in Finland and to the Middle East via the World Health Organization.

This review raises some important questions for your company:

1. Could the company increase profitability by manufacturing more custom specials, or is it wiser to concentrate on standard products?
2. Could the company reduce costs and improve performance by encouraging more effective consultation between designers and shop floor operators?

3. Does the company make fullest possible use of value engineering to produce profitable high quality products at competitive prices?

4. Is the company properly balanced between the components it manufactures and those it buys in? Is the company either bogging down making items that could be bought in more economically or is it buying in so much that it is becoming overly reliant on suppliers?

5. Has the company tried to visualize the next big consumer or industrial trend to see whether basic products or services might soon require major modification or replacement by a new generation to maintain profitable share of the market?

What Have We Learned from This Chapter?

- In the course of progressing toward a center of excellence, spare resources in skills, knowledge, or sources of funds will come into existence.
- These resources can be used to incorporate ancillary activities.
- Overconcentration on core activities is likely to be an unprofitable waste; defining overconcentration means another fine judgment.
- Guaranteed availability is always worth the cost to keep customer loyalty.
- Subcontracting part of the manufacturing process is needed when speed to market is essential, in this case with the object of leap-frogging ahead of competitors.
- In many products design is of overall importance.
- Service industries will usually provide service in-house unless they contract out to specialists.

In sum, companies as expert as Carbolite will normally create the total product in-house except where contracting is to companies with an extra special expertise. Normally manufacturing companies that are establishing a reputation as a center of expertise will produce as much of the product in-house as possible except where doing so would mean an unacceptable additional investment or the acquiring of especially scarce resources.

Chapter 10

Design

The appearance of a machine is a promise of its performance.

the late Viscount Mills
one-time chief executive of Avery

Key figures in any center of excellence are the designers. In the manufacturing industry they provide a vital element in production and in marketing. The designer has the power to make a product that is easy for the customer to use and, in the case of engineering products, easy to maintain. In marketing, the designer works out a product that is attractive to the market and is stimulating to the buyer. The designer comes in on the large scale for product design and (a different species of designer) on a small scale with the production of logos, emblems, and other contributions to the corporate image. Attractiveness to the consumer should also be listed among the requirements of design. Train equipment, cars, and buildings are just some products that need to be pleasing to the eye.

For the service industries, designers play a variety of roles from the appearance of transport undertakings, books, and hotels to retailing outlets and educational establishments where corporate images provided by designers are all-important. However, no one should imagine that corporate image is valuable if it does not promote a substantial corporate reality. This brief dogmatic statement refers to the fact that exaggerated promotion often refers to a poor product. The gap between image and reality is an accepted problem.

So what particular expertise or inspiration can be willed upon the designer? It is easy to list qualities that must be obvious to everyone's imagination, tempered by a shrewd commercial sense. The latter is a reminder that designers must be willing to place profit and loss considerations beside all their proposals. Fast-talking and temperamental designers have been known to persuade a board of directors to plan against their better judgment only to find out that "better judgment" was right after all. A more common, if less well-known, problem occurs when the designer's imagination is effectively suppressed by the administrators. The secret in this, as in so many similar issues, is budgetary constraint. If a daring new project is accepted, the maximum losses must be within the company's ability to pay both for the project losses and for the move to an alternative route. A good project manager or designer must not be penalized for losses incurred once a "daring new project" has been approved. That must be the responsibility of the board which sanctioned the expenditure in the first place and which, in any case, should be looking for new projects as long as they do not wipe out the company before they hit the market.

NEW PRODUCTS: TECHNOLOGY-DESIGN-LED

The notion of technology-led is now being replaced by technology-design-led.

P. Gort, *Design Management*

To maximize potential "relies on good communication and shared goals." This suggests that "good" design relies upon the eye of the beholder.

"Silent design" is the name given to a lack of recognition that past managers placed in the design process, the assembly of design teams, and the control of their activities. Many companies do not have a "design manager" as such. They employ consultants briefed to update their designs. A production manager incorporates these designs into the programs, hopefully with success.

Nowadays the stress is on the need for each project to be tailor-made. Satisfactory industrial designs cannot be taken off the peg. Design focuses on markets—as the market changes, so should the design. Arguably design belongs to marketing rather than to production, moving away from concentrating on what worked yesterday to what will sell tomorrow.

If the company is to be "product-design-led," the marketing department staff will demand a considerable influence. They will be researching the different appearances and attached emblems. The excellence of the product design, along with the image of the company, are all-important for the company's marketing program which cannot be separated from its design strategy. A famous failure where the design was separated from other considerations has been inherited from what was once British Rail. The company appointed a designer with overall control of design for rolling stock. She, the person appointed, decreed that each train should be self-sufficient, so that there would be no ugly corridor ends to allow staff or passengers to walk from one train to another if two trains were joined together to increase capacity at busy times. On lengthened trains this meant that many of the customers could not reach the buffet and that the ticket inspectors could not check the whole train. Now, it is claimed, each of the small privatized companies are putting resources into design to distinguish the trains of one company from those of another; but this "design" has more to do with paint work than fittings. In either case, the high quality designer leads a team that only gives of its best when left some latitude, a liberty that too many firms are unwilling to give. The emphasis is on quality and that must come first. The board must always retain the right to refuse a budget for a project that is not affordable.

Most companies use design to give a message about their products or services and to differentiate them from their competitors. There is an easily recognized message in appearances ranging from cheap and nasty through comfortable to luxurious; in the case of hotels the list is much less simple and nastiness does not necessarily match price, a reason for the popularity of so many hotel guides.

The "message in the design" can be as subtle as it is well known. In the retailing, leisure, and private motoring markets, for instance, improving design is thought to be a sales winner, only it must be understood that the price and the standard must roughly match. Consumer organizations have frequently pointed out that their researches do not always bear out the marketing maxim: "You get what you pay for." On the contrary, you may pay a high price for an inferior service.

We assume that anyone using this book as a guide will be interested in giving excellent value for money. The only departure from that principle will be in circumstances that the market will not bear a price that matches production costs. The corners may need to be cut, but an urgent research program needs to be put in hand to restore the cuts which must, in any case, be limited to meet an urgent crisis.

THE DESIGN DEPARTMENT

The contribution of the design department can be beneficial in two ways. For those inside the company, it can promote unity giving employees a sense of belonging; for those outside, it provides a distinctive image, a set of symbols that differentiates a firm from its competitors and tells customers with whom they are dealing.

Without the need to search for new products the design expert searches for innovation in other ways—to use the design capability to improve existing products, to make the case for design proposals by improved skills of communication, and to make the most of the design potential.

Company A, in the engineering sector, found itself in the doldrums. None of its products excited the market. In despair, management hired a design firm to promote a new lease on life; after this, business began to improve. The company learned, what many people have been saying: that good design is a great competitive tool while the process by which design has its effect is complicated. It can be useless to appoint a designer and tell him or her to carry on with a job already started.

Management must build up a design culture to supplement the culture of innovation in which those concerned feel themselves involved in the design process. Most companies that we have investigated do not have anyone who can be recognized as a design manager, not forgetting that most engineering managers also have design responsibilities. To designate a design manager may be regarded as a first step toward liquidation but, more hopefully, it will prove to be a move toward design excellence.

A recent "survey of hospital accident and emergency admissions" in Britain, summarized in *The Observer* newspaper (London, July 26, 1998), showed how new products could be stimulated by design faults. The report listed some ordinary and innocent-appearing household goods that had caused accidents serious enough to require hospital treatment including flower pots, crochet hooks, zip fasteners, and (most extraordinary) cotton batting.

The Sale of Traditional Designs

Museum managers have already discovered that reproductions of traditional designs or artifacts produce saleable products. Vintage cars and obsolete railway equipment come under this heading. The success of hobby steam trains has already made it likely that replicas will be needed to meet the demand. Indeed these, such as the Rocket and other pioneers, may stimulate a whole fresh demand. The growth of theme parks, an important contribution to the tourism market, is already exhausting the stocks of preserved vehicles. A businessperson looking for an outlet for some surplus capital or the opportunity to start a new firm need look no further than the local museum. The Victoria and Albert Museum in London has already licensed a number of businesses to reproduce their artifacts. What a chance for the new product development manager! The resulting replicas will make good exports.

CUSTOMER-LED INNOVATION

The report at the end of this chapter is from a spring company making components for the aircraft industry. A small supplier to very large purchasers.

Consider the enormous cost of a modern jet airliner built to fly with complete safety over thousands of hours; there is little wonder that so many of its components have to be perfect in every detail. This paramount safety factor is the spur behind customer-led innovation at Recoil Spring Company Ltd.

Located at Redditch in Worcestershire, England, it employs only twenty people and its sales turnover is £1m ($1.5m per annum). The company manufactures a wide range of extension springs, compression springs, torsion springs, sectional wire springs, and sundry wire shapes. The latter includes cargo door clamps.

The company is on the third tier of supply to the aircraft industry which means it supplies the manufacturers of subassemblies. The applications of its springs range from subassembly parts for the maintenance of the few remaining DC3 Dakota aircraft, so successful as a military transport in the war against Hitler, to the umbrella-type spring to aid the opening of the modern parachute. Today's aircraft are laden with a wide variety of springs of all shapes and sizes needed in subassemblies from the enormous landing gear to the smallest servo mechanism operating in flight control.

First, wide variation occurs in the basic metals used. This affects the tempering and hardening processes to be sure of the necessary high standard of duration and performance. Second, the accuracy of its dimensions and perfection of performance over long periods have to be guaranteed. The manufacturing operation, therefore, is mainly carried out by hand and work is 100 percent inspected and tested. Because of the exceptionally high standard of quality, its products are expensive. A fair profit is earned on this £1million per year ($1.5m) sales turnover.

Within the company a small subsidiary, Staymount Ltd., makes a stabilizer for caravan towage. This is designed on the traditional leaf spring principle following the original Scott invention. The insertion of a small spring which broke the Scott patent landed the company into the stabilizer business before it (the patent) expired. The company sells its products mainly to other suppliers of caravan equipment, for example, SAS (Safe and Secure) of Bristol, England.

What is to be the future innovation strategy of Recoil Spring and its subsidiary, Staymount? The first obvious path is to seek new markets. In what industries other than aircraft and parachute manufacture is there a demand for such high quality expensive springs? If that additional market is found, how can a twenty-person hand-making operation measure up to it? Can it acquire a bigger share of the aircraft market? A $1.5m sales turnover, albeit highly profitable, can only represent a very small share of "springs for aircraft worldwide." Likewise, can Staymount find an extension to its market? People always fit a stabilizer to a caravan to stop it pitching and swaying behind its towing vehicle. From this it follows that it is as desirable to fit a stabilizer to all types of small trailers, especially those used for carrying horses, cattle, and sheep.

The average price for a traditional leaf spring stabilizer is around £50 ($75) ("leaf-spring" so-called because once the parts are put together, the spring looks like a leaf). Some caravan owners, however, are prepared to pay £150 ($225) for a newer ball-grip ALKO-type device which performs well and is very simple and convenient to use. Can Staymount come up with a new type of device with all the benefits of the ALKO at less cost?

ALMEC DESIGN SERVICES LTD.

Success in Design

Gas is supplied to both industrial and residential buildings for heating and cooking in various parts of the world. All too frequently one hears of an explosion caused by a leak from a gas pipe. Consider, however, the constant risk of a fire reaching the gas meter, usually located at the point where the main supply enters the building. The resultant conflagration would be devastating, but today this hazard can be eradicated.

Design engineer Brian E. Shawcross, principal of Almec Design Services, designed a valve that will automatically close off the gas supply to the meter the moment the fire approaches the meter.

Mr. Shawcross did not get his brief for this design from either the gas supply company or the manufacturer of the meter. It came from another designer who judged Brian to be one of the most expert people in the design of this sort of device.

The first of Brian's principles in achieving high quality or high performance design is to make use of the best possible specialist expertise in the relevant product area.

For example, one of his long-standing clients, Gripple Ltd., had a stress problem with an item of the basic product line, the Gripple wire joiner. Each of two strands of wire are inserted into the opposite ends of a small metal lozenge-shaped device to be held securely by a roller bearing holding each into a wedge. The product is in use all over the world for wire fences, wine frames in vineyards, in building constructions, and in many other applications. In one case the Gripples were failing due to being used at a load well beyond the design capacity. There was a huge market potential for this application providing that the strength could be increased without increasing the manufacturing costs. Brian identified the areas where stresses were very high, but needed expert advice to verify his theories. For this he called on the services of a qualified stress engineer who used his finite element analysis skills to help determine the most efficient shape for the casting within the high stress areas. As a result, the strength of the Gripple was increased by 98 percent without increasing the weight of the die-casting.

A cardinal principle of good design, therefore, is not only to be able to design effectively within one's own sphere of expertise but be ready to turn elsewhere for design skills beyond the usual.

Brian finds that small companies can rarely afford their own designers, but in-house design staff are not uncommon in larger businesses. The latter must avoid becoming stale on the job, looking inward and trying to solve every problem and create every new design themselves. By doing so, they could seriously restrict their company's innovative ability. They have to be encouraged to shop around and find other designers who can add specialist excellence to their own general skill. During the 1950s, a leading British carpet manufacturer and a printer of greetings stationery both nearly reached the point of bankruptcy. Their sales had plummeted because their respective design directors had refused to consider ideas and suggestions from outside their own firms.

This leads to a second cardinal principle. Brian Shawcross's message to industry is never to lose the pioneering spirit. Businesses should always maintain a flexible attitude toward innovation and overcome any reluctance to change. Certain companies such as car manufacturers are forever pioneering and changing because their customers are continually awaiting next year's models. The outerwear garment industry is the same; dealers are agog to see the new season's collections. Outerwear fashion, however, is estimated to turn a full circle in twenty years. Other firms, which have a strong line of products selling well year after year, are inclined to settle down to routine marketing and selling. Their innovative activity is restricted to modifications and improvements to keep the line freshened up and in front of competitors. Brian strongly advises businesses to maintain an aggressive and bold quest for new products even if the existing range is reaping adequate profit expansion and growth. By bold, he means be prepared to experience a 10 percent failure rate in the design stages of a range of new products. Failures always produce valuable lessons that can be usefully applied to future projects.

Brian is a qualified engineer who was a tool designer in his early years. This background enables him to be constantly aware of the factors of manufacturing feasibility while working on design.

His design speciality seems to center on small intricate mechanisms. The standard iodine-filled bulb sprinkler system is inadequate for the protection of modern huge warehouses stocked to the roof with pallet loads of valuable goods. To cope with fire in these premises one needs a high pressure gush, not a sprinkle. There was the need for a sprinkler which is as sensitive as the standard device, but able to withhold and release when needed an enormous pressure of water. Brian designed a heavy-duty sprinkler for this application based on the valve being held in place by a strong trip switch mechanism which would give way as soon as the presence of fire was sensed.

Another of Brian's design projects has been in the realm of a basic domestic utensil—the mop. A mop comprises a handle fitted into a socket beneath which is a cup, down from which hangs a mass of strands of absorbent fiber string. In this case another designer, whose specialist expertise is in plastic moldings, designed the socket-cum-cup. Brian designed an automatic assembly machine to fasten the strands of string into the cup. Basically, the cups are placed in a conveyor socket end downward—cup end upward. The strands are in the form of a rope twist running above the cups the length of the conveyor. When each cup reaches the work station, a plunger presses the rope into the cup, forming a loop; a clip is pressed across the loop to hold the strands into it; the rope ends are cut off and there is a mop requiring only the handle. Domestic mops have been around for hundreds of years. Today they are made in an automated plant, the work of two designers.

From time to time designers are called in by companies experiencing fluctuations in their workload. These are usually where a service is provided, such as sheet metal fabrication. In these cases, the designs are limited to the manufacturing skills and equipment available on site so that products may be manufactured for retail during times of low activity.

The third cardinal principle upheld by Brian is the need for the designer and client relationship to be based on complete honesty and openness.

The client knows the industry, the customer base, the authorized budget for the project, as well as the targeted volume, the price the market will bear, manufacturing feasibility, storage, packaging and dispatching factors, and all the other restraints. There will inevitably be tenacious arguments between designer and client. Such dialogue is constructive in that it leads to the design which is most effective and takes into account all relevant factors and limitations. According to Brian, if two people always agree on everything, one of them is superfluous—a point often made—although in different words—in the course of this book.

When considering manufacturing factors, the designer can often prompt and guide the manufacturer to buy subassemblies economically from outside. This can be a wise course to avoid the expense of additional plants and labor until the new product is selling in a worthwhile volume. Designers, by reason of their work with a number of firms, often have a wider knowledge of manufacture than that of the client.

The fourth cardinal principle is to make the product "look the part." In other words, make its appearance give the assurance of its capability of doing the job for which it was designed. When shape and appearance are important factors, Brian makes wooden models of a device before getting into its mechanical design. If the function is of paramount importance (for example a subassembly to be fitted into a machine) he will fabricate the design in his workshop by hand with raw materials.

As an aid to the selection of materials, Brian sets up Material Property Charts. All the materials under consideration are listed down the margin of a paper. Property headings are set out across the top of the paper: costs, flexibility, hardness, combustibility, durability, weight, water resistance, and all the other properties applicable to the product. He awards points to each material under each property. Totaling up he has a reliable guide to show which materials are likely to be the most suitable.

Brian's fifth cardinal principle for successful design is to look back on obsolete techniques and to try to apply them to a modern function. While working on a problem with the Gripple, which secures barbed wire, he discovered that the method he used to strengthen was similar to a method used in the nineteenth century.

His sixth cardinal principle is that manufacturers of consumer and consumer durable goods should test products through a consumer panel before they are launched. This action not only safeguards against flaws unseen in the process of development and manufacture, but will often create an inflow of good suggestions for improvement and for widening its user applications.

His seventh principle emerges from his experience as a design consultant before establishing Almec Design Services in 1990. In this capacity he has witnessed client and designer lose control of the budget in the early stages of a project by mutual failure to ensure that the client does not commit expense until he or she is sure of getting good value for it. Instances of over expenditure on research and development are legion. Nothing can be more discouraging to innovation than to find the budget used up and nothing to show for it. This happens frequently when a project is funded by a grant from government or under European Union administration.

Let us conclude by summarizing the principles.

1. Do not be tied to one designer. Obtain excellence by using the best possible specialized expertise for the innovation project concerned.
2. Never give up pioneering. Always maintain a vigorous bold new product development program. Be prepared to accept and learn from failures.
3. Maintain complete honesty and openness in the relationship between the client and the designer. Let positive argument convey you to the best solution.
4. Make the product "look the part."
5. Look back on old obsolete techniques; they could be the solution to a modern problem.
6. Never launch a consumer or consumer durable product until it has been tested by a consumer panel.
7. Stay on budget track. Be sure you get value for money at each stage of development.

"For every problem there are many solutions and for every solution there are many problems" (Information supplied by Brian Shawcross).

What Have We Learned from This Chapter?

- The designer has a crucial role in giving the product or the service an attractive, customer-friendly design.
- The designer has to be constrained by commercial considerations and must achieve a workable balance between stimulus and constraint.
- Design is important in differentiating a company from its competitors.

- The design culture needs to match the firm's culture of innovation.
- Make use of the best possible design expertise (need to avoid overlooking design specialists outside the firm).
- There is a need for complete openness in relationship between designer and client.
- The designer needs to make the product look the part.

Chapter 11

Technical Research

Technology made large populations possible; large populations have made technology indispensable.

Joseph Wood Krutch

Many a despairing executive has said, "Half my technical research expenditure is wasted; the trouble is I don't know which half."

The bewilderment (despair) no doubt gives rise to figures often quoted in the press to show that research expenditure by British companies falls below that of other industrial countries. For example, an article in *The Observer,* Business Supplement (June 28, 1998), listed the percentage increases for research and development in 1997. The international league table might alter if a means of quantifying research in service industries, especially retailing, had been discovered. Many more resources, in cash as well as personnel, are available for retailing and other service industries. Complacency in this sector is dangerous. The figures quoted in the press showed the United Kingdom (at 5 percent) as low by normal European practice and half the international average among the top 300 international companies. The article also pointed out that the research and development expenditure varied considerably by industry sector. The article had a perceptive title—"R and D is not an end, but no R and D is the beginning of the end" (*The Guardian,* London, June 28, 1998). The top companies on the British list are in the pharmaceutical sector, predictably because their products soon become obsolete and they depend on research for new products. A chilling thought is that research is the first department to be axed during cutbacks or after a merger.

Nevertheless, most companies look to research departments for the new products when they know they need them. Throughout this book other sources of inspiration and vision are specified, but a department dedicated to innovation does exist, at least in the larger and in the technology-oriented concerns, even if the department is only lodged in the mind of the entrepreneurial proprietor in the one-man businesses.

THE RESEARCH AND DEVELOPMENT DEPARTMENT

The department is a luxury usually affordable only by medium and large companies. It is a staff function to support all the executive effort needed to create a new product or service from the original idea to the marketable result. The focus of the department's mission is in the technical field of the industry concerned. For example, in a food manufacturing business, it will contain experts in dietetics, edible colorants, chemical analysis, cooking techniques, and preservatives. The department might be headed by an experienced chemist or food technologist. In the tool industry, the department is likely to be staffed by metallurgists, experts in edge geometry and ergonomics, designers, and people experienced in metal-forming techniques such as casting, hot and cold forging, and shaping by lathe. The leader of the department would probably be an experienced engineer.

In a smaller company, the functions of research and development are likely to be contracted out with other research and design consultancies on a paid assignment basis. In companies large enough to afford a research and development department the board must make sure it is well supplied with qualified people and good equipment but cannot afford to let the department become a kind of holy cow.

Excellence

Considering a company that is striving for excellence and supremacy, the leader of research and development must be large-minded enough to know when the department needs help from outside. A good example is that of a company making fastening bolts for use in highly stressed applications in extreme temperatures, both hot and cold, as well as in space and in deep oceanic work. The problem was that some of the bolts were cracking after only a short period of use. In spite of the presence of a metallurgist in the department, the leader turned to a person holding a metallurgy chair at the local university. The professor found that the fault had nothing to do with the research department. The problem was that the bolts were being turned too fast on the automatic lathes in the factory. The lathes ran marginally slower and the cracking ceased.

THE PRODUCT DEVELOPMENT COMMITTEE

The product and development committee is also more usual in medium and large companies; it is convened to screen ideas and monitor progress. Members of this committee come from various departments of the business. They are *not* there as representatives of their departments but are selected because of their ability to make a strong impact. The chairperson, possibly the chairperson of the company or the chief executive, knows the innovation policy decided by the board. The member from the finance department will know what funds are available for innovation and how to get more investment finance if an excellent idea is going to cost more to develop than existing liquidity can afford.

A member would be drawn from senior manufacturing staff to judge on production feasibility of a new product and the magnitude of investment required for an extra plant or for machine modification. The committee is usually convened as frequently as necessary. Its agenda should be first to make an overview of all development projects in progress, the queue of new ideas waiting for appraisal, and a review of priorities. Second, it should examine new ideas and suggestions and authorize recommendations to the board for the development of those showing realistic promise. Some ideas are sent back for refinement or modification while others will be recycled. The third item on the agenda is to check the progress on all authorized projects with the appropriate project group leaders who should appear before the committee with their critical path analysis updated.

The project group is a team with a mission to get an accepted idea, be it product or service, launched onto the market in saleable form. The group is staffed by selected employees to make an innovation project happen and this work is usually in addition to their everyday duties.

As an example, let us assume that a micrometer manufacturing company has decided to develop a jumbo micrometer to achieve absolute accuracy on very large objects such as ships' screw (propeller) shafts. As performance could be a greater criterion than marketing, an up-and-coming engineer could be appointed chairperson or leader. She or he would select the team in conjunction with the director to whom the group will report. This could be the chief executive or the chairperson of the product development committee. The members of the group may include a member of the research and development department to ensure technical input; a factory foreman, who has been earmarked for future promotion and whose function would be to organize manufacturing feasibility; a member of the accounting staff to keep the project on budget; a member of the export sales staff to plan the marketing and selling which would take place mainly abroad.

Project groups are good testing grounds to measure the leadership and other abilities of aspiring employees. Although this chapter is about innovation, it is necessary to be aware that project groups can be formed to operate effectively in other disciplines.

For example, in the 1960s, a multidivisional U.S. manufacturing concern found itself in a muddle over the use of capital funds. The executive vice president set up a project group to create new procedures for the allocation of capital, criteria for return on investment, the setting of priorities, and the assessment of results.

Reverting to innovation, in a small company the project group could consist of one employee as chairperson, with the members drawn from outside, including a member of a supplier's staff, a consultant, an overseas agent, and other outsiders likely to benefit from a new successful product or service.

The research and development department has been the subject of a large literature which asks some broad questions, including:

1. How is a research department stimulated or constrained to promote the company's objectives?
2. What results can be expected and over how long a time period?
3. How and by whom can a set of criteria be established in the light of which these questions can be fruitfully answered?

STIMULATION AND CONSTRAINT

The first question, the stimulation or constraint of research and development departments, has been much debated. In the past, firms have been disillusioned by discovering that a research department has been set up which allows the scientists appointed to pursue their own interests without troubling too much about the profitability of the firm. This arises from inadequate briefing. Some research into the truth of this allegation has confirmed it, some has not, showing that a particular sample demonstrated a strong bias toward the objectives of the firm. Be that as it may, modern control systems and methods of management are not sympathetic toward individuals who pursue their own interests without sufficient regard to the firm's concerns.

It is often questioned whether research is a proper activity for a business firm at all unless it is narrowly aligned with company objectives. Research, it is assumed, is best left to universities where it is supported by public funds. Our job in business is to employ a small, high-powered team to scan the literature and keep in touch with current research and innovation, vigilant to identify anything that might be useful to us. A center of excellence in the company may be a waste of money and, if we are to establish one, our company must be so dependent on new technology that we can use anything that comes out.

Arguments about recruiting and retraining a research team of the highest excellence will continue, no doubt, until the end of time but meanwhile this chapter sets out the probable compromise to meet current conditions.

At least one well-known company, a household name because of its consumer goods, widely recruited scarce engineers for its research department. Many of these did not survive with the company when economic conditions made cutbacks essential. This is a common story.

The problem of retraining skilled researchers can be met by providing terms and conditions of employment that make it hard to leave. These may be expensive for the company but they are less costly than any probable alternative. Meanwhile the planner has always to remember that the development work is far the most expensive part of research and development and this has to be undertaken by a company wishing to bring to market new products competitively. In a manufacturing firm, the engineers needed are those who show particular skills at translating research into development and an ability to build a center of excellence into providing the company with new products for which the costs of research have been minimized.

Efforts are frequently made, for instance by citing international comparisons of research activity against profitable output, to persuade businesses to record higher levels of profitable output. The conclusions about this are derived, to put it mildly, from slender evidence.

In sum, new product development through technical research is likely to mean:

1. Identify a product where your company's skills could be most profitably employed (the "vision").
2. Decide how new this new product is to be or to what extent it will be a modification of an existing product.
3. Identify a source for the required product (internal or external: university, research institution, consultant) always remembering that useful outputs from such organizations will only be obtained by a narrow and clear brief.
4. Negotiate a budget with the supplier and a profit-and-loss account with the firm's internal auditors.

Make sure that this process is thoroughly worked through and, if the results are clearly positive, go ahead quickly.

The criteria for taking these decisions have already appeared but, at the risk of some repetition, they can be listed as follows.

- They fit with the existing products; check with the marketing department whether the market planned for the new product is one with which it (and especially its sales staff) is familiar.
- Check that the budget is realistic in view of the costs of development and promotion.

The following quotation goes to the heart of the matter.

> They must float up and down with the tide. The anchor problem must be mastered. Let me have the best solution worked out. Don't argue the matter. The difficulties will argue for themselves.

This directive was addressed by Winston Churchill (then Prime Minister of Britain) to the Chief of Combined Operations on May 30, 1942, for the creation of the so-called "Mulberry Harbors" required for the invasion of Normandy on June 6, 1944, two years later.

This directive exemplifies the spirit and crispness with which a company chief executive should be able to commission technical research by concentrating on the objectives. It is also a classical strategic statement: "Don't tell me it won't work; it must."

In a business, be it a one-man enterprise or a large corporation, technical research must be tackled as an executive responsibility, not a staff function. Under these conditions, the head of a research department, the research and development department, becomes a line manager responsible for motivating staff to produce targeted and agreed results.

A business may be glad of the benefits of broad research such as finding a fuel to replace oil when world resources have dried up. It may eventually profit from the findings of pure research such as analysis of and experimentation with tomatoes, in search of medical properties. Unless the business is a large company vitally dependent on such research, it cannot afford to tackle it alone. It may, however, subscribe together with other companies to the work being carried out by a university or other institution.

Technical research needed for new product development by any size business can vary in its complexity and scope. It could be a matter of: the retaining nut has to be completely immovable by the vibration of the machine. It must, however, be instantaneously removable to gain immediate access to the feeder tube in the case of blockage by a foreign body, probably a mechanical problem. Alternatively, it could be that the device must record 1,000 hours of television programs automatically selected by the recorded habitual viewing preference of the user. (The Ti Vor box was featured in the *Mail on Sunday*, London, September 19, 1999.) This task will involve the use of the highest technology in the field of electronics and would be long and complicated.

It is the duty of the chief executive or a director to whom the task is delegated to decide on technical research tasks, delegate them to researchers with terms of reference and time limits, budget them, and staff them.

The chief executive or the director of research and development reviews the product development program and the budgeted investment. As a result, decisions are made about the technical research projects needed and the order of priority for tackling them.

His or her next task is to allocate funds for each project from the agreed new product's overall investment, draw up budgets, and obtain the approval of the board. The delegation of project work has to be done simultaneously with the selection and appointment of research staff. If the research project is to be carried out internally there can be several ways of staffing it.

First, if a research and development department exists it can be delegated to one of the members of the department. Second, it may require expertise with which an employee in the factory, the engineering department, or the tool room, is already endowed. For example, the plant maintenance manager may have a specialist knowledge of fluid control, needed for a project concerning a new automatic leverage system. He or she can be asked to lead the project as an additional duty, possibly earning a one-time bonus for a successful outcome. Third, under the supervision of an experienced member of the research and development department, the project can be set up as a training exercise for suitably qualified trainees even, in some cases, the apprentices.

Likewise, there are a variety of ways of farming the project out. First, outside specialist consultants may be used. This can be expensive but, if a good selection is made, results are obtained without creating a queue or backlog of work in the research and development department. In its heyday before the onslaught of Southeast Asian competition in the 1970s, Stanley Tools in Sheffield placed all its edge geometry research work out to a metallurgical specialist in cutting edges. The quality of the results, the speed of progress, and the relief of the burden on the research and development department offset the cost.

A second way of placing research work out is to assign the project to a company which has renowned expertise in the particular field. The advantage of this method is that eventually the company shouldering the research work could be the supplier of the component or subassembly concerned. For example, if the machine under development requires moving joints, the manufacturer can approach a firm renowned for its temperature control techniques and ask it to undertake the work. When the research is complete, the temperature control firm can supply all the subassemblies for which the machine manufacturer has neither the knowledge nor the plant to produce.

Hand in glove with the appointment of internal staff or external consultants, the research project must be firmly delegated to them.

The director must spell out exactly what work has to be done, when it needs to be completed, the expenditure limitation, and the frequency of meetings for progress checking. All these factors must be agreed upon with the leader of the research project. In both internal and external arrangements it is essential to solidify confidentiality and security.

It has been said that the footsteps of the farmer are the best fertilizer. The spirit of this proverb applies to technical research. All engaged on a technical research project need to feel they are both wanted and well led. Without hindering or interrupting progress, the top brass of the company should visit the research team frequently, showing enthusiastic interest and encouragement.

There are many different degrees of sophistication through which research and development can be organized in a company and fed through to production. The crucial element, mentioned previously, is the link between research and marketing, with research asking the question: If we develop this can you handle it? Marketing then replies with feedback from its customers, present and probable.

The thrust of this chapter is toward research with an obvious payback. Only research, and still more development, will absorb resources which might be directed toward more immediate concerns.

In conclusion, let us return to the opening sentence of this chapter; it is necessary to find out which half of technical research expenditure is essential and we do this by examining the likely results.

Let us take an example from the railways in Britain. An institution called the Strategic Rail Authority (SRA) has been called into existence but, just to demonstrate that no one in Britain (or anywhere else!) really believes in strategic planning, an institution with a long-term title has been given a number of short-term ("useful") jobs to do. Its objectives have been defined by the chairman of the SRA, as "to enable more passengers and more freight to travel by rail and to ensure that they get a better quality service" (Speech at "Rail: The Full Picture"; Conference organized by the Waterfront Conference Company, London, 2000). Part of that "better quality service" is safety. Hence the SRA should be spending its money on long-term research into safety rather than frittering it away on short-term reopening projects.

KEY ISSUES

1. Innovations depend on people but those people must be enabled to work within a system that provides adequate stimulus as well as control (see Chapters 2 and 8). The fashionable expression "empowerment" is relevant in this context. Researchers need to be "empowered" with some freedom of research but be subject to clear objectives and schedules. (For example, "You must produce a new type of steel or a substitute for steel by June 2010; that instruction should be given to more than a research engineer in more than one organization." For more detail see Brooke's forthcoming book on the *Revival of Britain's Railways*.)
2. Research and development as a separate department will only exist in large companies. In smaller firms the function will exist in someone's head.
3. Simple explanations of metallurgical problems need expert investigation.
4. A product development committee is used to screen projects and progress on them; the staffing of this committee needs careful thought to ensure that the necessary skills are represented.

As a report on diversification to end this chapter, we print a brief study of a firm for which the development of new products is essential by the nature of the business and the demands of the customer.

GQ PARACHUTE LIMITED

Long-Term Projects Under Pressure

Mainly in the field of rescue, safety, and aerial control, the range of uses to which parachutes are put is vast:

- Emergency escape from a wide variety of fixed and rotary wing aircraft, including gliders
- Ejection seat escape systems fitted into military aircraft

- Low-level dropping of troops from aircraft flying at a height below radar detection level
- Steerable assault parachuting for covert military operations
- Steerable parachuting for displays
- Braking and deceleration of jet aircraft
- Recovery from faulty maneuvers in flight testing
- Recovery of unmanned aircraft and other items of flight hardware
- Aerial delivery of weapon firepower (for example, the German "land mine" dropped by parachute during World War II, a technique still used in modern warfare)
- Aerial delivery of supplies, cargo, and rescue dinghies
- Aerial suspension of flares

The common uses are increased by other less known functions. For example, small parachutes are packed into the tips of the sails of electricity generating windmills. If the control mechanism should fail and allow the sails to run free, the parachutes at the tips would open and halt the rotation. Another use of the parachute is the sea anchor to prevent a boat from drifting at sea.

Commitment to Innovation

GQ Parachutes Ltd. is a division of the Alchemy Corporation. It has been manufacturing parachutes since 1934 and has two sister companies. One is AML Ltd. which manufactures several delivery systems and air transportation equipment. The other is Para-Flite Incorporated which specializes in RAM-AIR Parachute Technology and is a major supplier of specialist parachutes to the United States Department of Defense. This trio of businesses constitute the leading manufacturers of parachutes worldwide.

The company has been committed to innovation throughout its history. It developed and provided thousands of static line chutes for parachute troops in World War II. Postwar it has not only kept abreast with ever-increasing demands for improved reliability and performance of emergency, escape, safety and survival, and military systems, it has also anticipated future criteria by foreseeing the evolution of aircraft and military requirements.

A Precision Flying Machine Launched from a Crushed State

GQ must take into account two cardinal factors in its innovative effort. The first is that a parachute is basically an advanced flying machine derived from a minor perturbation, along a random route to a predictable state. Successful design and manufacture of a parachute demands the achievement of accurate performance by a product made of inexact materials, often a complexity within a simplicity. For example, at low speeds the need is for the parachute to open quickly, yet the tendency is to open slowly. At high speeds the opening must be tempered against the inherent fast opening so as to prevent exceeding the man's physiological limits.

The struggle for accuracy and reliability of performance is intense. Textile materials must be shaped and joined to a tolerance of 3 to 5 millimeters. Constant change occurs in materials selected for different performance criteria and design. In operation, some parts of the parachute are designed to stand greater stress than others.

In the field of ram-air, high glide parachutes, a continuous demand exists for acceptable openings from 500 feet up to 36,000 feet. Various mechanisms are used to temper the otherwise explosive opening tendencies of such a parachute.

The sequencing of multistage systems frequently needs to be choreographed within millisecond accuracy.

The cause of parachute failures can usually be traced back to lack of discernment and perception of the performance requirement or to inadequate packing or training techniques.

Traditional methods are being complemented by vacuum packing techniques that have several advantages. The smaller pack causes less obstruction and discomfort in the cockpit. Little or no movement of components occur within the pack. No atmospheric damage takes place, such as through high humidity, as it is airtight. There can be no contamination and maintenance is reduced.

Long Term in a Hurry

The second factor is that a new product can take three years to become an active project and five to seven years before it comes on the market. Despite this apparently slow rate of generation, however, the number of projects in demand is so great that there is the same sense of urgency in GQ innovation as is normally seen only in a fast-selling consumer goods business.

Parachuting Engineers

GQ's innovation program has solid support and encouragement from the parent company within an agreed financial budget. GQ Parachutes has a strong research and development team of eighteen people led by the director of engineering who, in addition to his engineering qualifications, is an experienced test parachutist. Besides designers and engineers the team contains experts in safety and stress analysis.

Although the department is under a permanently heavy workload, it frequently must change its order of priority, occasionally due to circumstances beyond the company's control. For example, the advent of the Gulf War created a demand for the immediate supply of a special weapon delivery parachute. The workload has to be constantly assessed against budgeted funding. Projects from time to time have to be put on the back burner or ditched on becoming obsolete by an even newer development need.

Members of the research and development team operate away from base when testing prototypes under airborne conditions. Among other instruments a high-speed video camera capable of recording 100,000 frames per second is used to study the conduct of the equipment. Previously this had to be done from photo-film.

The testing of prototypes is carried out mainly in the United States, where GQ finds a liberal approach toward cooperation, stable weather conditions, and good availability of drop zones.

The pressing problem in GQ innovation is recruitment of research and development staff. On one hand, they need to find people old enough to be experienced in their specialities; on the other hand people have to be young enough to be skilled or become skilled in the sciences of parachutes.

Marketing

Sales are directed primarily to government agencies. The sale of parachutes for private and club flying and club parachuting are carried out via the Internet. This is proving successful.

The Electronic Lifesaver

In conclusion, it is worth reporting the innovative development of the Reserve Automatic Activation Device by GQ Parachutes. Its prime function is to activate automatically the main parachute and a reserve parachute in the event of a partial or full main canopy malfunction, based on altitude and excessive rate of descent. The authors hope that this will be of interest to any readers who are active parachutists.

The outstanding performance of GQ Parachutes Ltd. raises some questions for readers to consider.

- Does our company have either a history of, or a commitment to, continuous innovation? If not, what changes should we make?
- Do we have the right mix of specialists and experts in our research and development team or consultancy?
- Is our research and development team staffed adequately for the present and future workload? (Ideally we would like Jacks of most trades and Masters of several.)
- Do we provide our research and development department the best tools and instruments for their work?
- Do we ever try to forecast our customers' business or industrial innovations and to prepare our new products in advance to be first in with their requirements?

Chapter 12

High Tech

All too often, personal computer software companies burn brightly for a short period, raise large amounts of money in initial public offerings . . . and then "flame-out."

Financial Times, July 1, 1998

That quotation is to the point because hi-tech companies attempt to be at the forefront of new and exciting technologies.

What people ought to feel threatened by is that their business is being transformed—not by Bill Gates, but by a worldwide revolution in technology. (*Financial Times,* 1998)

The much-hyped topic of the technological revolution is the subject of a massive output of books and articles; the information technology industry is generating huge quantities of information. This chapter will not repeat that; it will examine some of the commercial issues which are dominating the industry and its need for diversification.

During the years 1997 to 1999 most months showed a record of attempted takeovers or sales brought about by the demands of high technology. While this book was being written, the authors heard of one famous company which sold its best known subsidiary on the grounds that it could not afford the costs of keeping the subsidiary's main product up to date, let alone develop new products of equal quality. This example, albeit of an anonymous company, illustrates the enormous expense of sustaining and developing high-tech products.

For manufacturing companies, the obvious route to new products is moving toward state-of-the-art technology. This is surely a credible national policy as well as one for individual companies—to complement military orders with products that improve the environment: Water purifying, waste disposal, medical machinery and other similar technologies are still in the process of development.

Press reports have been claiming that the British are falling behind other European companies in developing so-called "green technology," destined to be the big seller in the twenty-first century. We do not have sufficient evidence to say dogmatically whether this is true or not, but general knowledge tells us that a huge reservoir of expertise in the armaments and machine tool industries exists which can be available in other fields.

In 1998 a conference of major companies and the World Resources Institute confirmed the theme of the last paragraph by concluding that precautionary action was justified against climate changes and that the private sector can contribute to this "action" with flexible policies designed to match developments in the market.

A potential contribution of the public sector was identified in *Industry North West* in an article titled "Dynamic Partnership," which showed how a local authority (Pendle in Lancashire, England) was able to finance business usually classed as "high tech" while playing host to rapid innovation in computer hardware. Much of this was produced by small companies ever vigilant for a gap in the market. The large and much publicized fortunes are being made in software rather than in hardware. The desk top (or personal) computer manufacturer has diversified by using chips that were ever faster in the central processing unit. Once the 386 chip was considered the peak of development toward high speed and high tech. Soon this was replaced by the faster 486 which was made obsolete in its turn by the Pentium chip soon to be replaced by the Pentium II and then the Pentium III. Meanwhile the competition, Apple Mackintosh, moved rapidly to the speedy G3.

A related diversification occurred when a Californian company produced a telephone that can surf the World Wide Web. If you are into electronics, or even if you are not, the hungry market for new devices is well worth researching; gaps may still be found.

Simpler adaptations of high-tech products will establish themselves in the marketplace. Certainly, no simple routes exist to capturing high-tech market share. Speed and pressure are vital and the simpler adaptation route is also the safer.

Readers of this book will be more interested in a push forward into the highly profitable unknown, but the medium-sized company needs to limit the risk and how far it can leap must depend on its ability to absorb any losses along the way. A large concern, on the other hand, is well advised to keep resources for major innovations while employing experts to identify the most viable objectives. The motto for the high-tech diversifier is: Look to ways of starting up new products without going bust in the process. Budgets must include rapid and saturation promotions.

Some firms have a high-tech potential; other firms do not have it. If a firm has potential, it has certainly hired first-class outside consultant expertise or recruited some high-powered engineers or chemists to ensure that it keeps its place in the market. By definition, such a firm will be under great pressure to produce new developments at frequent intervals but, as long as the technology is in demand, it will have no doubt about the direction in which to seek the developments. Company research is not designed to interest the researchers but to keep abreast of the market—a market that will soon run away (and be lost) if trends are not matched. New vacuum cleaners or new washing machines will look much like the old ones, only they will incorporate new features which the customer will rapidly discover to be indispensable.

Most people regard the home computer as high tech. The very word "home" suggests an attempt at differentiation within the market, since the same computer is used in the office. This is constantly the subject of new product development. One of the present authors has demonstrated to himself the truth of speed claims by checking the time it takes to run a virus check for a 386 as compared with the same check on a 486.

Both the hardware and the software are being updated all the time and a new software package will make the old valueless. Wherever advanced technology emerges, a small improvement will make the old unsaleable, but the new will also be found to contain flaws which will, in their turn, be put right by yet another development.

Surely one of the most outstanding examples of new product development relevant to a large contemporary market has to be the announcement by a Belgian watchmaker of the production of a watch which sounds an alarm at the time of an Islamic call to prayer, always in local time, for the owner.

These examples have been drawn from engineering (microengineering!) but the biggest advances with their demands for new products can be found in the chemical industry (especially in the pharmaceutical subsector) and the related industries of food production and agriculture. The patient search for plants that contain ingredients for new drugs has been well documented but the important message to the executive is that new developments most profitably arise with products resembling those in which the firm already has a reputation. Credibility is the key to so much successful development.

This is the case with medical drugs where one product can make a firm's fortune (such as Zantac for Glaxo some years ago) until another comes along to replace it (such as Zoton). In the case of these medical drugs, a continual process of research is going on within firms and inside universities and research institutes which is partly funded by the pharmaceutical concerns. A process of further research is going on all the time in an effort to keep ahead of the field in this particular industry. In this case a specialty market consists entirely of doctors who prescribe although they are unlikely to handle the product. Other industry sectors do exist within which the person who is targeted by the sales representatives is different from the person who will actually sell or buy the product—theatrical costumes are another example.

THE HIGH-TECH MESSAGE

The message of this chapter, then, is that moving from one high-tech product for which the market is likely to disappear to another where opportunities are increasing rapidly is a case of high risk, leading (hopefully) to high rewards for companies that have coped with the risk; a simpler adaptation is recommended for those that cannot cope. If this is not available, the risk must be taken if the existing market is truly disappearing. The textile machinery industry is frequently being written off as obsolete but advanced technology is as frequently reappearing to keep some parts of the industry alive against all the pressures of world competition.

GOVERNMENT INTERVENTION

A final word to this chapter picks up the effects of government legislation to induce firms to devise evermore clever and skilful ways of avoiding coping with taxes and regulations designed to reduce pollution by making it costly. Germany has led Europe in diversification into antipollution machinery because of its tough environmental regime—a case of the diversification route map being a by-product of tax law.

Company X (an imaginary company to illustrate high-tech trends) has built up a powerful team of systems analysts and programs to keep ahead of the competition in the industry sector that it serves. Recruitment and training principles (discussed in Chapter 15) hardly apply to firms that have come to accept that, in their industries, labor turnover is ceaseless. Good software engineers, the management has convinced itself, will move around to profit by their scarcity value while they still have it.

Software engineers are scarce because all experts in advanced technology take around with them a saleable skill. Software companies have little difficulty in qualifying for another form of official intervention—regional grants for establishing their development.

High-tech–product progress needs hard thinking on the part of those capable of doing the required thinking. A profitable but elusive market is being served and great vigilance is required to remain in it.

The article "Why the antitrust cops should lay off high tech" (Barro, 1998), demands that government stay out of antitrust cases against computer firms on the grounds that change is so rapid and competition so intense in the industry that an apparently overpowerful position in the market may be rapidly overturned. Professor Barro asserts that Sun Microsystems Inc. is developing a system that may knock out the windows operating system. Whatever the arguments for and against antitrust actions, this example demonstrates dramatically the reality of threats as well as opportunities in high-tech business. For the threat to become itself an opportunity obviously means sustained and long-term investment in new products.

THE ST. JAMES'S PLACE GROUP

The financial services market does not lack potential. People generally are underinsured, underinvested, and underpensioned. The financial services industry however operates in a cutthroat, over-crowded arena where many competitors are being forced to eliminate their direct sales forces because they are not viable, where products can be so similar that tackling competition on price is rife. Consumer and other protective government regulations often place added burdens on the players. To survive, one has to expand. To expand requires the highest standard of leadership of a team of top quality people with a steady flow of new products to get their teeth into. The St. James's Place Group claims to be doing just that.

Clear Business Objectives

The company's mission statement is "To be the most professional and trusted provider of advice in personal financial services."

The target audiences are professionals running their own businesses or in management roles in large organizations. They are people in the "higher net worth" category, who have a clear understanding of the types of product and service they need and are expecting the best standard in terms of advice and subsequent benefits.

The benefits the St. James's Place Group offers to its clientele fall into three main categories:

1. Creation of capital for the future
2. Management of existing assets to maximize capital or income
3. Protection against financial risk

Sound Structure

The St. James's Place Group was founded in 1991 under the name of J. Rothschild Assurance Group. In 1997, St. James's Place Capital Plc. became the parent company on merging with J. Rothschild Assurance Group. In June 2000, the Halifax Group, a one-time building society that is now a bank, bought a 60 percent interest in the parent company.

Strong Performance

In the year 2000, St. James's Place Capital Plc. recorded pretax profits of £80m ($110m), before exceptionals, a 33 percent increase on the previous year, on sales of £185m ($257m) an increase of 42 percent. This performance was described by a leading London stockbroker as "a stunning set of new business figures."

A Thrusting Partnership

The St. James's Place Group provides a wide and expanding range of high quality financial services. They are marketed and delivered in the United Kingdom through the St. James's Place Partnership, a group of 1,050 highly skilled and experienced financial advisers.

The outstanding feature of the strategic philosophy of the Group is to delegate all activity to people and organizations who have expertise in each speciality.

To ensure the best possible return on their clients' investments, all fund management is subcontracted out to a select number of respected and successful specialist firms. Clients are assured that this is "delegation" not "abdication." The Group has one investment performance monitoring committee, which examines the performance of the fund management firms every quarter. If a firm fails to deliver the standard of achievement expected of it, their clients' funds entrusted to it are removed elsewhere.

Likewise all the back office administration is delegated to another company to leave the ten-person executive management team free to concentrate on marketing, sales, and innovation.

No Ranks Between High Command and Front Line

The 1,050 self-employed partners are directly responsible to the chief executive, Michael S. Wilson, for sales. Their remuneration is by commission.

Before being accepted as partners, they have to prove their capabilities. They must have a minimum of three years experience of high performance with a successful financial organization; their previous earnings must have been above £37,500 ($52,000) a year. Moreover they must have had a proven track record of productivity and determination.

The company has a policy of "no hiding place," which means that every partner has direct access to the chief executive or any other member of the executive management group. Partners meet once a year at a day-long conference in London to discuss strategy, especially new products and services. The only form of sales publicity is personal recommendation and investment seminars.

The care of clients' investments and the administrative function, are both delegated to people outside the company. The reader will realize that this high-caliber leadership frees up the partners for new product thinking.

Both the chairman, Sir Mark Weinberg, and the chief executive, Michael Wilson, have headed and been responsible for a successful financial services group elsewhere before creating the St. James's Place Group. The quality of leadership is evidenced by the enthusiasm of the partners.

The Product Range

The products and services offered by the Group are:

- Proactive financial planning
- Retirement planning
- Investment planning
- School fees planning
- Tax mitigation
- Income during disability
- Capital following critical illness
- Offshore investment and offshore protection planning
- Shareholder and key man protection
- Residential and commercial mortgages

All over the world, financial organizations compete fiercely with each other to deliver these and similar products and services. Not only is the battle fought out frequently on price, but the battlefield is strewn with obstacles in the form of statutory rules and regulations.

In the opinion of the chief executive, the success of the Group is primarily attributable to the high quality of its partners. To enable them to perform even better there has to be a continuous flow of new products and services.

Innovation

It is vital for the company to be quickly responsive to changing customer needs and aspirations. The partners, says the chief executive, are a superb channel for client feedback. For example a client may call on a partner to discuss a particular investment need to suit a change in personal circumstances.

While the situation is unlikely to be unique, the partner will report the clients' request to the executive management team. From this, they may be able to devise yet another new product or service. If their decision is affirmative, the new item, arising from the clients' original request is put into shape and its availability circulated to the partners. Getting them all to grasp it with immediate enthusiasm is one of the tough tasks in making the innovations work.

In 2002, the Group added general insurance and possibly medical insurance to its range, through joint ventures with specialist firms.

The principal innovative venture has been entry into direct banking through the connection with the Halifax Group. This move will include the current banking initiative of encouraging clients to couple their indebtedness, including property mortgage, in one account with their earnings and savings. This can create substantial benefits to clients.

The St. James Place bank is an innovative step, albeit with help from the Halifax Group who have already successfully entered general banking. It still brings the business face to face with a new set of experienced and established competitors both indigenous and from abroad. They may have to cope with preemptive strikes by entrenched opponents. This venture needs an important factor of good quality leadership—courage.

The Group claims to select quality people. It decided to concentrate on a clientele of successful people. It entrusts its clients' funds with top-ranking fund managers, to whom it has delegated the task of producing the best returns. Every customer and prospect is under not only expert but conscientious care of a competent partner. In this company the idea is that the leadership concentrates on leading. The management is delegated out to others.

This gives rise to some questions for the reader to consider:

1. Is our company aiming at the right level of clientele?
2. Does the quality of our products suit the level of clientele?
3. Is our feedback on new product and service opportunities from our sales and marketing people good enough?
4. Are we studying these ideas well enough to develop new products and services from them?
5. Are we failing in our cardinal tasks by cluttering ourselves with matters which could be done better when delegated out?
6. Do we envisage our next big innovative ventures?
7. Do we have the skill and experience to handle them?
8. Do we have the quality of leadership and staff to make our plans happen?

Chapter 13

New Products by Branding: Basic Industries

For generations, the British have developed a taste for a brand of apple known as Cox's Orange Pippin. No doubt there are some people who march into a grocery and ask for "two pounds (or one kilo) of apples." More likely they will ask for Cox's. The most dedicated fruit eaters will take some persuading to recognize that "Cox's" are the same fruit as other brands of apple. The same will be true of other fruits and farm products in all countries. It cannot be so long since the milkman will have been asked for "a pint of Jersey." Health scares have changed all that and he or she is more likely to be asked for "fat free, please" nowadays.

The following is an example of the value of branding. In the maintenance hangar of one of the world's largest airports, there were two batches of Phillips type screws. One was packed in boxes branded with the manufacturer's name; the other batch was packed in unmarked plastic sachets. Workmen needing Phillips screws invariably insisted on the branded pack although the screws in both batches were identical.

You may be in a business sector that does not allow product innovation (if such a sector exists). You may have to achieve the same aim, in the way farmers have always done, by *product differentiation*. There was an interesting and relevant piece on the branding of sand in *The Guardian* for June 13, 1998, ending with "But why stop at sand? There's a whole unlikely world out there—you can even brand wheat, bricks, metals, concrete . . ."

But "product differentiation" is not the whole story, as we shall see shortly, the setting up of enterprising arrangements between units in basic industries—"strategic alliances"—is an even more profitable way forward. It leads into the short-term results for which we find ourselves under pressure.

TREES AND FOREST MANAGEMENT

Forests have turned into a sensitive subject since the middle of the twentieth century and not one where you would expect to look for product innovation. After all a tree is a tree is a tree is it not?

The answer to that is "no" as a recent article in a United States business magazine demonstrates (see *Business Week,* May 3, 1999, article titled "The future of forest products" in a "special advertising section"). The article points out that with modern technology trees can be felled, and replaced (using genetically modified seeds employed for an increasing range of products). The article ends in a bullish tone: "In the October 1998 *Atlantic Monthly,* it is argued that 'The model for the next Industrial Revolution may well have been right in front of us the whole time. A tree.'" We agree.

BASIC INDUSTRIES

The industries upon which wealth and employment have long been dependent have an equally long reputation for ingenuity in introducing new products.

This is especially true of agriculture. No one can earn a decent living in industrial countries by producing milk and wheat while masses face starvation in the preindustrial nations. Long-accepted principles of economics are seen to be irrelevant to this problem. One hesitates to step in on a subject which European negotiators must have debated for long and sleepless nights, but a remedy would seem to be obvious even to economists in rich, industrial countries: find new crops. Any incentives to this appear to produce only a perpetual problem: over-production which lowers prices to a level that no longer earns a living for the farmer. The answer, surely, is to put subsidies into product and materials research in the hope of finding new products. This partnership of primary producers with researchers and inventors in advanced branches of chemicals, materials science, and engineering may be a pattern for other industries threatened with the difficulty of finding a niche in a changing and unforgiving business competition.

Ask yourself: Would my company do well to forge such a partnership?

Take a fresh look at your apparently humdrum products and dream up a new one, a new fast-growing hardwood for instance, if this is biologically possible, of course.

Behind every commonplace product there is scope for innovation and improvement. This book, dedicated to New Product *Vision,* should never leave anyone content with serving out the same products for ever after. New products in many basic industries will come through development in the laboratory or in the experience of the operator—a development that needs to be market led. Abandon the idea that the market for coal as an industrial fuel will ever return. It has become a basic chemical and the mining company needs to see it in that light. This may suggest a small output of coal to a large output of chemical, it certainly suggests a concentrated research effort, if only to identify another chemical by-product.

Coal and metals industries have also found help from such forms of collaboration with research companies. Although it still seems unlikely that by-products of coal will support the production of even one mine, the search continues for more efficient means of producing smokeless fuel. Oil and gas are in a different league, still capable of making fortunes, it seems, in spite of international competition for markets and worries about pollution.

CROSS-INDUSTRY ASSOCIATIONS

A way forward for the agricultural, and probably other industries, is a series of a consortia of farmers to fund research for new materials made out of new crops. This could provide a viable pattern for progress, making worthwhile the search for a coordinating initiative. Even if government assistance is needed, the cross-industry association is likely to be a more cost-effective approach than direct subsidies to farmers. The pharmaceutical industry could be asked to provide assistance in new materials research.

The research might be carried out by chemical industry experts or by experts in materials science. What is needed is a series of projects carefully targeted and with strict time limits. Research departments or organizations do not need an incentive to spin out the investigations. We repeat a fundamental principle from the last chapter: research projects must be disciplined by time schedules and budgets.

How are these budgets and schedules to be fixed? The answer brings us to a theme of this book: negotiation. Both management and the scientists or engineers in the research department will have their own ideas about how the research should be carried out. Management needs to calculate the minimum time considered feasible and the maximum time considered advisable. Managers, for their part, will need to calculate a maximum time considered reasonable while also determining a maximum time allowable. The negotiations will be over fixing a date which comes between the minimum and the maximum for each group, although each may wish to consult an outside expert before entering the negotiation. The cost of the outside expert should not be included in the budget.

CODEMASTERS

Founded in 1986, Codemasters rocketed to 400 employees in Britain in fifteen years. Sales and distribution offices in Germany, France, Spain, Benelux, and the United States added to the employee total. In that fifteenth year (2001) sales reached £59m ($88m). The previous year the company had won a Queen's Award for Enterprise for innovation.

No surprise, then, that Codemasters is into electronic games; one called "World Touring Cars." In this game, players experience the excitement and stress of racing high performance BMWs, Audis, Peugeots, Toyotas, Renaults, Volvos, and Nissans over the best-known racing circuits of Europe, the Americas, Australia, and Japan as well as Codemasters' home country. The electronic drivers must cope with all the hazards of high speed, jostling for position, overtaking techniques, scrapes, wheel locking, collisions, and crashes, as well as the personalities of individual world famous drivers.

A vast amount of work goes into the creation of such a product. Every famous racetrack on five continents must be thoroughly photographed, not only generally, but also through the drivers' eyes of a wide variety of cars in motion. The exact behavior of each car, suspension reaction to bumps and undulations, the pitch of sound in various gears, the tilt and the rock need to be recorded with complete accuracy. Even the aftermath of a crash in terms of debris and wreckage must be realistically depicted and all of it shown in an accurate three-dimensional presentation.

Another product, Colin McRae Rally 2.0 is a revision of a previous rally video game. It features six cars racing head-to-head over eight unique looped circuits through majestic scenery with changing weather conditions. Players can experience cracked spoilers, back bumpers broken off and dragging along the ground, shattered windscreens, and all the hazards of top-rank driving.

The same realism is injected into another product: a football management game, LMA Manager 2001, which is the first truly realistic football management game on console. It provides the contestants with control over authentic footballers from many of the larger English, Scottish, Italian, German, Spanish, or French football clubs. The player is able to control his team on the field, making tactical changes and substitutions at will. To create this game, Codemasters has had to make photographic records in 300 different stadiums in 32 countries and more than 8,000 authentic football players complete with home, away, and goalkeeper strips.

Alongside competitive games, and with the same creative zeal, Codemasters publishes the Music Series, leading home music software for personal computers on CD-ROM, and now for Playstation 2. This is a comprehensive, easy-to-use, and flexible music creation package spanning many musical styles. Its unique facility enables multiple players to join in a simultaneous music jamming session. It enables skilled musicians and composers to contrast or remix music tracks, and if they so wish, to add appropriate video graphics.

These are but a few examples of Codemasters' video games, which cover cricket, boxing against Prince Naseem Hamed, rugby football, downhill mountain biking, and many more best-selling games in competition against hundreds of other products throughout the world.

The product innovation challenge for the future is not only to develop and design new games but to keep them compatible with the rapid development of new platforms from which they are played. Existing examples of platforms are Playstation, the Internet, and even the mobile telephone.

The Culture of Excellence

Since the earliest days of the business, the founder directors continuously strive for perfection. As the company has grown, this has become a culture of excellence. Their employee recruitment procedure is thorough and discerning. Every applicant must undergo psycho-

metric testing as well as a series of in-depth and provoking inter-
views. The company knows the intelligence quota (IQ) of every
employee. Recently the company received over 8,000 applications
for a series of posts. More than 1,500 people were interviewed and
only seventy-four accepted.

Once accepted, the fortunate applicants are given good opportunities for career advancement; each one has his or her own personal development scheme.

For each game there is a team of about forty people ranging from
artists and musicians to technicians. Each team is structured for or-
derly management. The task is delegated to the team as a completely
planned project with a financial budget and agreed milestones of
progress.

The heads of these teams are directly responsible to the design and
development director for successfully reaching each target on time.
The chief executive concentrates on forward strategic vision and
dealing with serious problems.

As a creative project is being developed, the assurance of outstanding quality has to be obtained at every stage of the way, not only at
milestone checkpoints.

The company uses the quality assurance department as an important part of the creative effort. It is also an intensive training facility
and proving ground for employees judged to have potential for advancement to senior positions.

Every time the smallest modification is made in the development
of a video game, the quality standard and detail can be affected both
laterally and through the length of the game run.

The quality assurance department is a very busy and exacting part
of the business, sometimes working through the night to guarantee
perfection without holding up the creative process.

The Visionary and the Creative

In Codemasters the two parallel and integrated sides to the business, the strategic visionary function and the creative activity, are
managed by the founder directors.

All other facets of the business are the responsibility of the managing director, supported by the finance director, the sales and marketing director, and the commercial director.

This group of directors ensures a maximum standard of financial and general administration, human resources management, marketing and sales at home and abroad, customer services, licensing and security, as well as other management disciplines. Licensing and security are given special mention here.

Licensing

Many of Codemasters' games are supported by famous names such as Colin McRae, the rally driver, Prince Naseem Hamed, boxing champion, and the Toca car racing organization. In addition to these licensed properties, the company works with external development teams whose projects are compatible with their publishing portfolio. They help these teams from their own internal design and prototypal capabilities. Music 2000 is an example of Codemasters' product licensing procedure.

Outwardly the company licenses carefully selected partners to develop titles outside its own range and to take advantage of new opportunities.

One Problem: Intellectual Property

If security were lax, millions of pounds worth of intellectual property could be carried away from Codemasters' head office on disc in a person's pocket or briefcase. Security measures, therefore, rank high.

Unless told the exact location of Codemasters premises, you will not find it: there is no external directional signage. The main entrance appears to be the way into a farm (the building in which the firm started) and is signed up accordingly. To get into the complex, an employee must be identified four times: first by the guard on the gate, second on entry into the appropriate building, third getting into his or her office, and fourth before starting up the personal computer. Visitors also undergo these checks.

Hand in glove with the security of intellectual property the company is taking positive action to prevent piracy, the making and selling of illegal copies. The company has created a unique antipiracy system that makes a Playstation game gradually degrade when being run from an illegally copied compact disc. The company realizes that it will only be a matter of time before the "pirates" find the antidote, thus, work on further refinements of the system are in progress.

What does this mean for the reader? This overview of Codemasters' operation raises several questions for readers.

- Do we use our research and development manager and his or her team in a staff role to support line management in their innovative efforts? If so, would we get better results if this were a line appointment with direct responsibility for a successful innovating process and making it happen?
- Could our quality control function contribute more to nipping quality faults in the bud and getting quality standards firmed up in the course of product development?
- Are we missing growth opportunities through failing to study the scope for licensing at home and abroad?
- Are we aware of the value of our intellectual property and are we providing adequate security for it?
- Are employee selection procedures good enough for getting the best possible productivity?
- How near is the conduct of our business to a culture of excellence? Are staff being inspired to strive for perfection?

PART IV:
WHERE DO WE GO FROM HERE?

Part IV includes a number of specialist chapters not easily fitted earlier in the book. It includes a separate look at subjects such as special issues relating to service industries (rapidly becoming the typical employers in industrialized countries). It covers market research and relationships between companies and governments—a subject which, although forming a whole library of publications, can only merit a brief chapter here. After that, a very short chapter (17) titled "Failures" shows how to reduce risk. Part IV ends by bringing together some crucial issues by reexamining our main themes while looking to the future of new product development. Chapter 19 includes a brief note on business ethics as it effects new product development.

Chapter 14

Services

Nowadays the old prison has been turned into a hotel with service that any Michelin guide would be only too pleased to condemn.

Spike Milligan

Service industries have been included along with manufacturing throughout this book. However, but it is not always easy to discuss the two at the same time. This chapter concentrates on the special situation of service industries. Among these industries are retailers, transport undertakings, banks and financial institutions, along with patenting and many other agencies which include the established professions, such as medicine and law with rules that usually inhibited diversification until they were relaxed in the twentieth century.

It is common these days to hear representatives of service industries speak about their "products" but, on principle, their search for new customers is often in terms of innovatory practices rather than products. The two, products and practices, go together in, for instance, the strategic search of the established professions, such as accounting and architecture.

Accounting is an example of a well-known service industry. As they have grown and sought new products to provide extra income, the larger accounting companies have separated their consultancy function from auditing. Most accountants also provide consultancy services. These separate divisions specialize in management consultancy and exist as profit centers in their own right, thus making the consulting a new product. Many firms now report higher profits from their consultancy division than from their older established auditing departments; the results of these are improving, but consultancy is the less price-sensitive activity.

The older, traditional, professions have an image problem which some have been at pains to correct. Have they succeeded or have they made the problem worse? A partial answer lies in advertising where this is permitted, as well as in the retraining of staff to present a more customer-friendly approach. For all service companies there is a need to accumulate and codify experience, often hard-won. This is the service industries' equivalent of stockpiling, except that it does not show as a cost unless a major retraining program is undertaken all at once.

That would be a good subject for debate if your company is a legal or accountancy firm or an educational establishment; if it is another service or manufacturing company, the question is how to find an equivalent to stockpiling.

ACCOUNTANCY AND LAW

Increasing bewilderment with the tax system has provided accountants with a natural system for diversification, a more recent move into new products, for some accountancy firms. A major difference exists between corporation tax with its ACT (advance corporation tax) and the intricacies of VAT (value-added tax, the form of sales tax used in European and some other countries). Tax advising is a traditional product of the accountancy firm, which is confident of producing correct answers to questions about the different tax allowances for corporations and for value added tax in different countries?

A more recent move is into *real-time accounting,* as it has come to be called. A running system of reports (updated daily or hourly) provides current figures with greater immediacy than a record of what happened in the previous year. Instead, a system of continually updated accounts highlights recent trends. This significant diversification overcomes the old complaint caused by the requirement to assert that a company's accounts provide a true and honest record of the state of the business. They actually provided only an average "record of the state of the business" over a whole twelve months—months which might have seen startling changes made clear in real-time accounting.

Legal experts (barristers as well as solicitors) have similar specializations to accountants with whom they often have a close working relationship. Barristers' opportunities for new product development have mushroomed recently with the rapid increase of international business. With different interpretations of contracts cropping up in various countries, the chances have increased for diversifying and gaining a reputation for a special expertise—into contractual conditions in Islamic countries, for instance.

ADVERTISING AND PUBLICITY

Every so often the advertising industry is stirred up by a new *enfant terrible*—loud, rude and determined to blow raspberries at its elders. But even by Charlotte Street's high standards, St. Luke's comes on strong.

The Observer, August 28, 1997

This introduction to an account of one advertising agency is a reminder that advertising is a business sector that lives in a state of permanent new product development.

Stockpiling has already been mentioned. An obvious difference between manufacturing and service industries—that services cannot be stockpiled—needs to be emphasized again. Doctors cannot have a store of answers ready to provide for every ailment that might arise among their patients. Each fresh problem demands a detailed investigation and diagnosis. Only then can a doctor draw on a relevant consultant or a suitable supply of drugs if they are in the wholesaler's warehouse ready to meet the demand.

It is not impossible for a service organization to keep records of skills that are available but not currently in use; skills held by consultants can be recorded for use when needed.

THE HOSPITALITY AND TOURISM INDUSTRIES

The so-called "swing to the service industries" as the main employers is assumed to be mainly in holiday accommodation, restaurants, and pubs. In fact, the figures do bear this out; but along with this, other changes have occurred. Newspapers frequently comment on "the disappearing private hotel." Nowadays few people can remember the days when so-called "en-suite facilities" were confined to the more expensive rooms in the larger hotels or when flexible times and menus were not available for evening meals. The coming of the motel changed all that. It may not be obvious that a restaurant can change the national origin of its meals when it requires new products, but this happens with increasing frequency; chefs scan the world for new cuisine while drinks' suppliers (and buyers) promote international changes. Innovation in drinks usually means United States-style cocktails, while changing tastes in food have come from the increase in international tourism.

CHANGING TERMS OF BUSINESS

Let us now stop and look backward for a minute. Business is carried out in the future. It has little interest in the past, except to gauge progress from the obligatory accounts. Even if our eyes are always fixed on the future, there are lessons from the past that can help us to understand the present. Societies have undergone, or are undergoing, four distinct phases.

- *Phase one: The agricultural.* Predominant industry in ancient times.
- *Phase two: The so-called "industrial revolution."* This is an expression which summarizes changes in the world. The typical workman dressed roughly and worked in the fields until the nineteenth century when factories took over and overalls became the dress of the menial worker.
- *Phase three: The transition from manufacturing to service industries.* During a long drawn-out change from factory overalls to suits, factories have been largely replaced by the service industries led by the financial institutions. The typical worker of today wears a suit or its feminine equivalent. Jobs are acquired by qualifications and ability.
- *Phase four: The transition from services to electronics.* A new form of manufacture with products and uses handled by people in white coats and face masks has arrived with the electronic

age. The big markets (United States, Europe, and Japan) are all moving into stage three, and *this move is of critical importance to your business, whatever it is.* The first transition from agriculture to manufacture was happening almost unnoticed until the year 1851 when the British census of that year showed that less than half the population was employed in agriculture; this was the first country where that distinctive transition occurred.

SERVICES ALWAYS IMPORTANT

The service industries have been important throughout history. Two sectors in particular—education and finance—have met increasing demands as each stage emerges. The moral is: Don't despise the service sector in the search for new products. At least two of the world's largest companies have moved from manufacturing to financial services in their search for diversification. One (mentioned already in this book) is British American Tobacco, which is now a large insurance company as well as a cigarette manufacturer; the other, the U.S. firm International Telegraph and Telephone, also moved into insurance and then diversified further into hotels. Both of these companies are likely to experience more upheavals as the service halves seek to be divorced from the manufacturing and later to dominate it. ITT is, in any case, a modern electronics manufacturer.

From the beginnings of industrialization, financial services have been critical to progress. Other services have tended to grow rapidly with the economic growth set off by the factory system. Never forget that business generates wealth and that increasing wealth leads to greater demand for leisure pursuits, medical advances, education, and other services (including accountancy and law) that newfound wealth is willing to pay for.

Among recent indications of the rising importance of the service industries have been the nomination of the founder of a business consultancy as "UK Emerging Entrepreneur of the Year" (see *Business North West,* November 1999). Another example is the switch of GE (the United States' General Electric) once regarded as the champion and arch exponent of manufacturing (85 percent of profits in 1980) to a largely service company (75 percent of profits in the late 1990s). The increasing significance of football clubs on the British Stock Exchange is yet another indicator. Chambers of commerce are of different importance in different countries. In Germany, for instance, they play an important part in company law. In all countries where they exist, chambers of commerce play an important part in the service industry. One particular chamber which has diversified more then most is the subject of the new product report in this chapter.

SHEFFIELD CHAMBER OF COMMERCE AND INDUSTRY

The talent for innovation is not in any way confined to industry and commerce but also to various institutions ranging from hospitals to charitable trusts.

The present-day innovative activity of the Sheffield Chamber of Commerce and Industry has followed some 140 years of gradual emergence since its foundation in 1857.

Basically it has followed the same pattern of development of most chambers of commerce in the United States and Britain. This progress has been succinctly recorded by American business historian Steven Woolley and published in written model form by an American firm of business consultants (Foresight Dynamics, 2000).

The Paternal Chamber

Throughout the nineteenth century, chambers of commerce and industry were paternal in their function. Their boards, consisting of the heads of the largest businesses in the area, made decisions with minimum consultation with members—"We know what's best for our business community." Chamber activity was limited to trade exhibitions and promotions. The chief executive officer was the board secretary who controlled a clerical staff, in many cases poorly paid part-time employees, with consequent high turnover.

The Entrepreneurial Chamber

At the turn of the century and through the 1920s, chambers of commerce took on an entrepreneurial function. The chief executive officer assumed leadership. He was a full-time salaried employee who set the agenda for the board. He dealt personally with the heads of all member companies, took a hand in all committees, and was responsible for events and the initiating of new programs. He maintained liaison with other trade, industrial, and professional organizations and negotiated the chamber's wishes through local controversial issues such as civic objections to industrial development in a particular area.

The Professional Chamber

During the years following World War II, chambers of commerce became professional in their operations. The board, sometimes advised by a committee or council of members, decided strategy and established priorities for action.

Much of the strategic thinking in Britain was centered around reaction to government economic policy and counterbalancing the influence of the trade union movement. The chief executive officer became the official public spokesman and was responsible to the board for implementing its policy through leadership of the chamber staff as well as through outside contacts.

In Sheffield, the board comprised the president, the senior and junior vice presidents, two past presidents, and the treasurer. It has been and still is aided by a council consisting of some heads of member firms and representatives of other local trade, industrial, and professional institutions.

Staff became structured into departments with their managers reporting to the chief executive officer. Individual members of staff were specialists in particular areas of aid provided for members such as export documentation; certification of origin; the provision of export data including contact with government commercial representatives abroad; the contents of chamber bulletins; advice on the handling of trade infringement problems besides many other areas of consultation; and the organization of business training.

Getting its feet deeply into training was the beginning of innovative action in the Sheffield Chamber. From the middle 1980s and through to present times it has organized business training on two fronts: first, that funded by the government in an effort to reduce unemployment and, second, training paid for by member firms for the development of their employees. While it was effective in its purpose, the training initiative was a financial disaster, which almost brought the chamber to insolvency. Since then it has recovered, and today the chamber provides training in over fifty business subjects embracing all the main disciplines. Some of the courses are divided into several modules.

The Fusion Chamber

To appreciate the next development of chambers of commerce, as recorded by Steven Woolley, it is necessary to be aware of the large number of organizations trying to contribute to the growth of small and medium-size business enterprises. They include chambers of commerce, general and sectoral industry associations, employers' federations, educational institutions, banks, venture capital initiatives, municipalities, regional boards, and state institutions.

Since the middle 1990s, chambers of commerce have increased their effective influence to foster economic growth by fusing with other organizations. Such fusing is not passive representation on their boards, but active participation in their governance.

The chief executive officer of the Sheffield Chamber and members of the senior staff have direct involvement in twenty-one organizations in the city of Sheffield. All of these organizations are striving to improve the social and economic development of the city itself and the regeneration and growth of its industry. Though many Sheffield steel mills have closed, more steel is made in Sheffield today than ever, only it is done with far fewer people than in the past.

Two of the chambers fusions in Sheffield reflect the growth and promotion of other industries, which the city needs to replace the slimming down of steel and allied traditional industries such as cutting and tool making.

The Sheffield Chamber's chief executive officer is a member of the board of the Cultural Industries Quarter Board which supports 250 companies involved in journalism, creative arts, and tourism.

Among various initiatives with the Sheffield City Council, the chamber has become the owner of Sportslink (Sheffield) Ltd., which draws its staff from the council. The first purpose of this organization is to foster the rapid acknowledgment of Sheffield as a leading international sports center through the spacious stadium and other facilities created by the Sheffield Regional Development Board. Second, it is aiding the brisk development of sports industries in Sheffield such as the manufacture of ice skate blades, gymnastic equipment, javelins, track suits, and diving equipment.

Within the boundaries of South Yorkshire the chamber has fused with twelve organizations and eight more throughout other subregions of Yorkshire (England) and nationally. The speed of fusion with a total of forty-one organizations is in itself an innovative accomplishment, too broad to describe in detail in this review.

One innovative example has been the establishment of the South Yorkshire International Trade Center, the largest in Britain. This center is an operating unit of the Sheffield Chamber, supported by the chambers of neighboring towns: Rotherham, Barnsley, and Doncaster. It is staffed by twenty people and also involves both the universities in Sheffield, the Sheffield City Council, British Trade International, and the South Yorkshire Small Business Service.

The Center aims to stimulate regional growth by:

- Encouraging small and medium-sized enterprises which are not exporters to attempt to trade internationally.
- Enabling exporters, whose foreign trade is experimental or incidental to increase their international trade capability.
- Assisting companies to identify and access new market opportunities and new routes to various markets.
- Encouraging the use of new technology, such as e-mail, as a marketing tool within developing and expanding exporters.
- Increasing the marketing activity of firms individually and, where appropriate, collectively, through joint ventures, clusters, and networks; promoting strategic alliances in the region.
- Providing coordinated, targeted, flexible, and high quality support to improve the level of internationalization of South Yorkshire companies. Internationalization embraces exporting and importing as well as investment and establishment abroad.

To achieve this, the Center staff provides the following services to businesses:

- Advice and action planning both strategically and tactically
- Specialist market research
- Web-based access to markets in the form of secondary research, specialist research, and export leads

- International trade training
- Market visits including overseas and inward trade missions
- Financial support by helping to obtain government and European Union grants

The following are examples of achievements during its formative period, which augur well for the Center's future.

- Helping a manufacturer of material-handling equipment, who has only been a reactive exporter in the past, to obtain a £3m ($4.2m) order from Egypt
- Providing funds to an ice skate blade manufacturer, which is a brand leader in North America, to carry out research into the best route to profitable diversification
- Providing funds to a world-class exporter to break into the Japanese market, thus increasing sales from £50,000 ($70,000) to £1m ($1.4m) per annum
- Helping a supplier of highly specialized material-cutting solutions for the aerospace industry to consolidate its position as a major supplier to Boeing

The Sheffield Chamber today is one of the most effective and wealthiest chambers in Britain and is taking its member firms forward with it.

If one reflects on the slow progress made by the chamber of commerce movement up to the mid-1990s, one is reminded of Machiavelli's statement: "There is nothing more difficult than to take the lead in the introduction of the new order of things. Because the innovator has for enemies all those who have done well under the old conditions."

Another quotation, this time from a Japanese business professor, is to the point:

> You [Western businessmen] firmly believe that sound management means executives on the one side and workers on the other; on the one side are the men who think and on the other men who can only work. For you, management is the art of smoothly transferring the executives' ideas into the workers' hands.
>
> We are beyond this; business as we know, is so complex and difficult the survival of organizations so hazardous, in an environment increasingly unpredictable, competitive and fraught

with danger, that the continual existence of firms depends on their ability to keep changing through the mobilization of every ounce of intelligence.

Through its fusion with other organizations, the Sheffield Chamber is doing just that.

This review raises some questions for readers to consider:

1. In our approach to innovation are we outgoing or do we restrict our progress through being too inward-looking?
2. Among all the outside bodies, from our suppliers to our bankers, who could give us more help with innovation? How? Have we gotten close enough to them to take advantage?
3. Does our organization enable us to mobilize all the talent in our business?
4. Do we really haul in all the intelligence and talent to be found among our people?

What Have We Learned from This Chapter?

- The relaxation of rules in the ancient professions (such as accountancy) has led to searches for new products which provide more profitable innovations.
- Advertising is being used, as well as staff retraining, to improve the image of these companies.
- Real-time accounting has been an important innovation in the accountancy industry.

None of this is to suggest that manufacture is disappearing; the products will continue to be needed, all the more as societies grow richer. However, industrialization shifts the emphasis to services.

Chapter 15

Market Research

The new product must be brought to market and, before this, market research is required. The scope and scale of the research will depend on the size of the company and on the expected payback from the product. The formal activities of a professional market research company may provide responses as accurate as are available but will come outside the cost budgets of many companies.

As a rough guide, if formal market research is being considered, it should only be undertaken if the cost is not greater than the expected income from the new product over two years. Otherwise, the company should undertake a modest investigation. A test market may be more cost-effective in any case.

Customer sensitivity panels have been advocated as a reliable and cost-effective means of assessing the market. "It's amazing what they throw up," one enthusiast said of a technique which brings together panels of competent and experienced people to advise on new product proposals.

The marketing suggestions proposed by the research must be firmly tied to the proposed new product (*not* to one of its predecessors) and must fit with the company's existing marketing skills.

It has been argued that proposals suggested by any technique for marketing research may be made useless if the target customers do not know what they want. In this case, and especially for consumer goods, test marketing may be the most reliable form of research. This will be especially important in the case of innovations which are minor in the eyes of the producer (the same technology, a similar product) but do not fit with consumer perceptions of the old product: P. M. Chisnall (1992) illustrates this issue by the instance of Del Monte producing a yogurt that did not need refrigerating.

Another authority (G. E. Hills) identifies the following questions to help a company to decide whether or not to launch a new product:

1. Does this firm have experience in the market to which the new product will be directed?
2. Has the target market been identified and measured?
3. Has the competition been convincingly evaluated?
4. Has a market plan been evaluated to work out the new products' effectiveness?
5. Have the sales or market share been reliably forecast?

The same authority makes a neat distinction between entrepreneurs who are impatient of market analysis and their moneybags (venture capitalists) who demand more of it.

A news item in *The Observer* (October 19, 1997) described a rather special new product innovation following a very special market research. The country was Brazil and the company was Unilever, which launched cheap and cheerful soap products for the 80 million Brazilians the company had previously thought too poor to become customers. The market research included groups of managers living and working beside their potential customers and washing their clothes in streams alongside poor families.

Many companies that manufacture consumer products, as well as their suppliers, have a rough-and-ready rule of thumb to identify the limits of their market in terms of the average wealth of the local population. Calculated by the average gross domestic product per head, the calculation must be as localized as possible to make sense. The example of Unilever Brazil has blown a hole in such calculations by demonstrating that a market can be expanded to the benefit (hopefully) of a poor population and of the company. Whatever the opinions about this, the moral of the Unilever Brazil example is not to accept received wisdom on the limits of the market or the possibility of expanding into unexplored territory. The example also demonstrates the need for a process of education within a company as well as among its customers.

Customers thinking to follow the example just stated would be well advised to scan a publication of the British government: *Eliminating World Poverty* (Department of International Development, 1997). In the apparently boring eighty-two pages of this white paper, firms can gain a host of ideas for new marketing ventures in partnership with peoples often shunned by companies on the grounds that they are "too poor to bother with" (to quote the words of an executive of one of the world's largest and best known companies). Surely it is not cynical to suggest that the first sign of growing wealth in the poorest is likely to be a demand for consumer goods. Even if there are practical and moral issues concerning the direct exports of finished products, there will be a great demand for franchising and licensing agreements. These are new product developments for thrusting companies.

Market research is all part of the ongoing task of gathering market intelligence. By market intelligence we mean

- The changing for better or for worse of the acceptance of a product.
- The activities of competition in that product field in that market or their forays into new markets.
- The introduction of new or improved products by competition which threatens the sale of your product in any market.
- The changing pattern of distribution, such as supermarket chains closing down small retailers, or direct selling by mail order threatening both wholesale and retail trade as people start to shop on the Internet.
- Gaps appearing in all types of markets for something new to fill. These gaps are always occurring across the whole spectrum that can be drawn from consumer goods to technical electronic instrumentation.

Assume market research to be a specially mounted program of intelligence gathering to provide a report on circumstances governing a specific project, such as a new product.

If this is so, the more effective and efficient the day-to-day gathering of market intelligence, the less expense is needed for market research projects. The quality of a company's market knowledge can be so high that the additional market research can be kept narrow and less costly.

In the recent past, the gathering of day-to-day market intelligence has come largely from the daily and weekly reports of traveling salespeople and agents. Today fewer traveling salespeople are employed; their place is taken by telesales staff.

Intelligence, however, is still needed. There are still numerous sources including telesales staff, sales engineers, the trade press, the consumer and the user press, visits by directors to major customers and to principal suppliers.

Many a new product has been "leaked," as a result of a competitor's buyer discovering its label on a printer's floor.

- In the case of consumer goods, a sympathetic study of wholesalers' and retailers' sales and profitability aspirations and problems, by sales managers and directors.
- In the case of engineering and technical products, a sympathetic study of customers' technical and design problems by sales engineers and directors.
- The routine review of recruitment advertisements in the particular industry. Why does the Bouncer Spring Company want to recruit a metallurgist? Are its recruiters planning lighter-weight devices for heavier performance products or entering a new field of application such as underwater installations?
- Watching sales drives or special offers of competitors' products. Are the competition clearing out the market to make way for something new?

Let us assume therefore that our readers and their companies have got their market intelligence gathering into excellent shape and performance, before they spend money on market research themselves.

The concept of a new or improved product or service usually arises from clear and informed (by well organized day-to-day intelligence) forward vision. The cost of development is hefty and could therefore be a grave risk. The degree of risk or a warning against foolhardiness can be determined by market research.

Before the research program can be planned, a few basic facts must be determined to focus its aim.

- The influential party will eventually command acceptance of the new product or service by:

  1. the individual consumer
  2. the retail trade
  3. the wholesale trade
  4. the large manufacturers in the case of technical appliances
  5. instruments and components
  6. an engineering and scientific plant instruments and components distributor for small manufacturers

7. one's own government, for example, authorizing drugs for use in the health service
8. foreign governments.

- The size of the sample needed to give a reliable result. For the Kinsey reports on the human male and the human female the samples amounted to hundreds of thousands of individuals. The concentration of a moderate number of samples in a small area, or several small contrasting areas. Examining an industrially oriented city and a commercially oriented city could be more cost-effective than attempting a reliable sample over a wide area such as a whole state.
- The exact cardinal points you want to know: minimum accepted performance standard, maximum accepted price, appearance preference, design preference.
- Probable objections to buying.
- Main reasons for possible nonacceptance.
- Size of buying population, consumers, domestic, or business users.
- Economic standards (or ability to afford) of consumer, domestic, or business users. Determining these facts will enable a company (in consumer products, for instance) to crystallize exactly what it needs to derive from a market research project.
- Consumer field.

1. What quantity can we expect to sell in year 1, year 2, year 3?
2. What price can we get for it?
3. Which supermarkets will handle it?
4. What trade margins must we allow to motivate wholesalers and retailers?
5. Where will it sell best abroad? Do we need to prove it at home first before exporting it, or should we run a trial abroad first?
6. Can we and if so should we protect its name and label? If so in what countries?
7. What is the preferred packaging? (image, value for money); The options may be limited in Europe where there are controls on packaging.
8. What is the likely sales effect on existing products?
9. Is it important to clear existing products from the market to make way for the new product?

Once you have listed the facts you want to research and the questions you want answered, try out (pioneer) your trial questionnaire on, say, twenty-five carefully selected people. These can be drawn from staff, trade or user customers, suppliers, or coopted members of the public. This will tell you how to the point your questions are, which have little bearing, and should be removed, and which new questions should be added.

Now that you know exactly what you want from your proposed market research project, how are you going to get it? The method, size, and expense of a market research project varies from phone calls to the principal retailers to nationwide questioning of individual consumers or users by a specialist agency.

Within the scope of this book it is impossible to review all the methods available, but the following guidelines can help the reader to take the best "value for money" path.

1. Consider whether close knowledge of the business is so essential to the conduct of the research that it should be done by your own staff. On the other hand, could an outside market research agency obtain a clearer picture, unclouded by a fixed line of thinking from within the company? Maybe the task is best undertaken by an agency closely supported by company staff.
2. Consider the sensitivity of relationships between the company and its customers. A manufacturer of aircraft navigation equipment is likely to discuss future requirements more freely with a sales engineer from his supplier of printed circuits than with a member of a market research agency.
3. Take into account the experience of a reputable market research agency. Their acquired professionalism could extract the information you need more quickly than your own staff.
4. Remember that the market research agency is in business to make money. The best will never try to persuade you to widen the research beyond what is necessary, but they will press to go wide enough to ensure reliable findings. Therefore, you should keep a close watch on limitations. In this connection a small pilot research can be a useful way of testing the competence of an outside agency.
5. An experienced, well-respected outside agency can possibly modify your questionnaire still further, even after you have tested it in-house.

6. A pilot research by your own staff in a similar market overseas run parallel with an agency pilot research in a domestic market sometimes yields the most reliable results for least expense, as well as a strong indication of the road on which to continue.

With these guidelines in mind, the business feels its way to mounting a market research project. If the findings show good prospects for the proposed new product, all well and good. If not, the innovation project should be modified. Adapt in line with the market research findings or scrap it.

While market research is needed *before* the new product proposal is accepted, a consumer panel should be used *after* the product is developed and immediately *before* commitment to production. A consumer panel is a group of twenty to thirty people with whom the company is in close touch; they can be remunerated with free samples and similar awards and favors. The following are specimen comments.

- "It is amazing how often after all the design work, all the technical and market research, some silly little defect goes unnoticed until after the product is launched."
- "As a member of a consumer panel I found the vacuum cleaner excellent but another four feet of flex would make it so much more convenient. With the existing cord, I would still prefer my old machine."
- "The taste of the new salad dressing is indeed delicious, but why is it packed in a narrow-necked bottle? It is so difficult to get it out."
- "This component is always fitted in pairs, so why don't you pack them in pairs? It makes the technical storeman's job that much easier."

Chapter 16

Companies and Governments: The Hostility and the Emerging Consensus ("Poor Mr. Gates")

Pop stars worry about "paradise syndrome": the problems that arise from a surfeit of success and happiness. Superstar companies seem to suffer the same complaint. Witness Microsoft. Tragically, it makes too much money. The Seattle-based software house is sitting on nearly $9 billion in cash and short-term investments that earn a meagre 5.2 % return—about a third of what even an average firm would hope for as a return on capital. Sadder still to relate, without some creative efforts to spend it, that pile grows by $18m a day. ("Poor Mr. Gates," 1997)

The article in *The Economist* was headed, ironically, "Poor Mr. Gates." The article addressed the difficulty that a cash-rich and influential company had in trying to invest an ever-increasing wealth. Any attempt at takeover would cause trouble with the competition (Anti-Trust legislation) and it already had enough of this. Not long after that article was published, Microsoft scored a notable victory in court. The issue was whether Microsoft's "Internet browser" should be sold as part of a new software package or whether Windows Plus browser was a product in its own right. The court ruled that the latter was the case. Marrying the two products made a new product. Had the court ruled differently and asserted that the browser and the Windows Internet package were separate, as the prosecution claimed, the insistence on selling the two together would have been an illegal restraint of trade. As it was, the effect on Netscape and other competitors was irrelevant. Competition law, this judgment affirmed, could not be used to prevent new product development. So there you are. No need to worry about new product development clashing with competition laws, but you must prove that it is genuinely new product development.

The case exposed a severe problem in the relationships between companies and governments. On the one hand, governments see a need to hold the ring to ensure that a few powerful companies are not able to stitch up the market and prevent free entry. All industrial countries have now passed legislation forbidding overwhelming power in the marketplace. The progress of this legislation has been followed by a number of high profile cases on both sides of the Atlantic.

Problems in enforcing competition legislation have placed this high on the agenda of national governments and regional associations. In the European Union, a competition policy was put in place early in its existence and without much controversy compared to other measures. The reason for placing competition legislation high on the agenda of regional groupings arises from one of the problems that individual countries have in enforcing legislation when a large company that has mighty power in one market may have very little power when matched against international competitors. The rise of the global market means that many concepts have had to be redefined, notably the meaning of competition.

Competition law is a relatively noncontroversial intervention of government in industrial affairs (unless you happen to be a victim, of course) as are health and safety regulations although some would make the limits of government intervention narrower than others. These activities are the negative side of intervention along with labor and industrial relations regulations. On the positive side, all intervention is controversial, depending on one's political standpoint. Political parties, which are these days usually described as "center left," find themselves upholding government intervention in more circumstances than the "center right" parties, although these latter are just as convinced of the need for competition legislation as any others—free enterprise must remain free!

All of which leaves the assumption that business performs at its best in a free market without big government overlooking its activities. This is the normal view of modern governments, left and right. Assistance to small or new companies in setting up exhibitions at trade fairs, notably those abroad, is not usually disapproved especially by firms that might benefit from the assistance. Companies are likely to note the current national politics and delay actions until a change of government produces a more favorable atmosphere. Detecting the difference can be complicated as is shown by the example of France which currently (summer 2001) has a center left prime minister and a center right president.

An alternative view is that a government should pick winners, preferably in business sectors rather than in actual businesses, and direct advice or subsidies toward those sectors or companies. This view does not find much support in industrialized countries which aim to carry out business in all sectors, leaving competition to sort out the companies—which shall live and which shall die. There will be some of each; the role of government, in the normal business view, is that it should make sure that only legitimate practices are used to speed the sorting process.

Some developing countries, on the other hand, see trade controls as the only way to make a serious impact on world commerce. A problem is that the obvious sector for developing countries—textiles—is unsuitable. The industrial countries where, in most cases, industrialization began with textiles find it politically impossible to countenance any proposals against the interests of their own textile industries. Two developing countries do seem to have achieved successful industrial policies: Malaysia, with heavy engineering including motor car manufacture, and India with computer software. Both of these developed by a natural process. There was little specific government intervention to pick these sectors; that came later after they had picked themselves. The Indian example was the subject of an article in the *Financial Times,* on July 1, 1998, titled: "Indian success is a model for the region." The implication of the title is that the article lists other countries in the Indian subcontinent—Sri Lanka, Pakistan, Bangladesh, and Nepal—which are interested in India's progress.

In listing the measures that governments in the subcontinent have been or are taking to promote software businesses, the article shows the options that are open to developing country governments to influence trade. These include relaxation of import duties or controls, rewards to successful exporters, reexamining the national educational system to develop a new generation of software engineers, and encouraging foreign investment in the sources of a specialization for which the industrial countries are short of adequately trained people. However, these general principles do not determine the situation of individual companies or subsidiaries operating in developing countries. These may find themselves bewildered by the stop-and-go measures they encounter when attempting export trade with those industrial countries considered suitable for improving their national trading balances.

Every textile business in every type of country is apt to find itself caught between incentives and disincentives. It may be eligible for investment grants, especially assistance up to the limits permitted by the World Trade Organization. At the same time, their activities will be closely scrutinized to ensure that they are not engaging in tax-dodging devices or anticompetitive practices. A complaint often heard is: "We are encouraged to export a proportion of our products and then find ourselves in trouble when we actually do so."

Maybe you solve your problems by appealing to your government—the Department of Trade and Industry in Britain and the Department of Trade in the United States and equivalent departments in other countries. If you get no luck with this appeal, maybe your cause is hopeless and you are developing the wrong products for markets you cannot enter. Never give up the whole process, but be ready to admit defeat on one front to attack more fiercely on others. Nobody made a fortune by obstinately attacking hopeless markets or by giving up too soon. Since you are on the way to justifying your company's existence and your role within it, you need all the help and the allies you can find.

These thoughts lead on to the question of the fashionable arrangements known as strategic alliances. Since some of these so-called "alliances" are on the borderline of infringing competition laws, it is difficult not to believe that the expression "strategic alliance" was coined to make them sound respectable. In fact, the phrase covers a wide range of arrangements, from old-fashioned and long-accepted licensing and franchising agreements by which one company sells much of its operating information to another, treating twenty-first-century style knowledge as the most valuable product, to joint ventures in which two companies pool their investment so that each can make use of the special knowledge that the other possesses without actually merging. The most likely form of joint venture, and the one most likely to find itself on the borderline of competition regulation is forming an agreement without actually incorporating a new company. The whole question of strategic alliances is considered in Chapter 18.

A suggestion in Britain for government assistance to an industry sector is that of antipollution technology. Opponents of all government intervention will not accept this, but it has been suggested that Britain lags behind other countries in its sale of this equipment. An article in *The Guardian* (October 13, 1997) showed government support that could be called a limited intervention by providing some start-up funding to a company selling environmental technology and the establishment of a so-called Green Globe task force. It has been pointed out that many countries have strict antipollution laws which have forced industries to develop technology to match the laws, a technology that has proved highly saleable worldwide.

Even the most economically liberal governments are likely to bring pressure to bear on businesses that could contribute to national prosperity. The reverse of this, on the business side, is *lobbying*. The scope for individual companies to lobby government departments is limited to the very large firms in which some of the largest have appointed officers who fulfil a few of the functions of an ambassador. They may attempt to influence government activities at the same time as officials are trying to alter corporate policies. Smaller companies lobby through trade associations and other similar bodies.

Government officials are apt to be sceptical about business attacks on government initiatives. An example was that of the chief executive of a major international firm, who was running a high profile campaign against government intervention. At the same time, the executive frequently visited the appropriate ministry to plead for intervention to protect his industry sector against foreign imports.

A full discussion of the mutual influence of companies and governments is not relevant to this book. The point is that government influence—even if only brought to bear in an informal manner—may well lead to new product development. This may be a profitable development if the government has correctly identified an opportunity for the country in world markets.

The message of this chapter is:

- Do not worry about competition legislation unless planning a takeover. As a general principle, by the time the legislation hits you, you will be rich enough not to worry.

- Look for legislation which produces scope for new product development (in manufacture or in legal, accountancy, or other services).
- Watch for declarations of government policy, debates in the legislature, and statements by ministers indicating assistance for new products.

Chapter 17

Failures

The awareness of the ambiguity of one's highest achievements (as well as one's deepest failures) is a definite symptom of maturity.

Paul Tillich

This is an optimistic book, all about success and excellence. But we recognize that failure or disappointment does happen. We need a chapter that uses a few timely warnings especially when we have frequently advocated high risk. *All* of the book is about *high risks* undertaken to ensure holding the market against intruders by the simple device of carefully timed new product development. High risk must mean a high chance that something will go wrong. *New* product development may be very risky, but *no* product development is so risky that it will surely lead to failure.

The problem for us, the authors, is that failures do not usually hang around long enough for us to analyze them and draw the lessons. What we can do is look at the reasons given for failure. These also form well-known packages and it seems almost as difficult to fail as it is to succeed. Don't try: go for success instead, starting with your strengths.

Nevertheless, to repeat, taking risks does assume the possibility of failure. That is what risk means; we need to investigate the risk possibilities in every project.

Common advice suggests not to invest in a declining market. Beware of all common advice.

Naturally an objective review is needed to be assured that a market is really declining. The trouble is all too likely to be that it is the company's marketing that is in decline, not the market (see Chapter 3). Excellent market research or very shrewd judgment is needed for management to be assured that it is the market, not the marketing, that is in decline. So many examples have been seen in recent years of products that once appeared to be growing obsolete but have yet revived under fresh direction. Gas and railways are both examples. To promote part of the innovative products or procedures in a business sector previously thought to be declining is likely to turn out to be a very profitable investment indeed.

Millionaire Sir James Hanson earned his millions by concentrating on products which he regarded as time-honored basic necessities.

A subheading of the declining market is—we have already suggested—a failure to penetrate a changing market.

Never lose sight of our number one theme: an innovative company needs to form a staff package that includes vigilant groups and vigilant individuals. A theme running through the book—including recruitment and motivation—is the competitive edge needed for new development. Without a strong basis in all its functions, a company multiplies its risks. If every effort is concentrated on making the new product policy work, there is no space to expand resources on other possible projects which deflect from the mainstream. This is a well-known principle all too seldom implemented. Many firms seek profit today while ignoring tomorrow. Of course, this year's results must show a reasonable performance to give possible investors confidence in the future. The short term and the long term are not as mutually exclusive as many theories suggest. No one will assist in new financing for a company which handles its existing investment incompetently. Some boasts about "taking the long view" are no more than attempts to cover up failure in the short view.

Stop and THINK. Allow these messages to sink in and then realize how the resources of your company need to be brought together and allocated in priorities. The marshaling of the resources will include a fresh look at the factors that have already brought about innovation. Once the thinking is finished, the fastest action is required. The worst failure we have heard of was of a company that spotted an opportunity but failed to follow it rapidly enough.

One of the differences between British and Japanese management methods, it has been said, is that the Japanese spend longer planning a project and then act very quickly once a plan has been worked out. The British are impatient with formal planning and incur long delays because they cannot act decisively enough as a result of inadequate planning. Bad timing is a serious cause of failure. One is reminded of Lincoln's saying: If I was given six hours to chop down a tree, I'd spend five hours sharpening the axe.

RISK

Do not run around like a frightened rabbit in the face of risky situations. If it is risky to make a decision, it may well be riskier still not to make it. In early 1999 the British food company Booker Plc., struck an acute liquidity problem. This problem had crept up gradually but became obvious by the end of 1998. A merger was carried out, intended to retrieve the situation, but the company had lost the confidence of the city and the shares were bumping along on their bottom level. The institutional shareholders stepped in and a new top management was appointed. At the same time, a new financing package was negotiated which gave the company a breathing space by postponing the repayment of loans whose timing had precipitated the crisis. Booker was a large, well-established company; it is not so easy for small firms to negotiate "new financing packages." For them, the experience of insolvency may be an important lesson in management after which they will be able to rise to a successful future.

During the previous year, an office equipment company (Danka Business Systems) had come into difficulties in a very competitive market and also found that interest payments were taking up too high a proportion of the company's revenue.

A valuable way to help cope with failure is to devise an "exit" tactic to minimize loss. For example, a pilot launch will cost less and be easier to abort than a national launch. Decide in advance how the material stocks of a failed product can be used elsewhere. Cigarette making is one industry in which this is easy. One minimizes the quantity of packaging to that needed for a pilot launch. Then, in case of failure, only the cigarette-making machine print wheels and the packaging are written off. The paper reels and the tobacco content can be used elsewhere.

A report in the *Financial Times* (August 14, 1998) suggested that the problems of a firm under examination were caused by the difficulties of integrating two sales forces after a recent merger. The problem of low interest cover was also mentioned.

Chapter 18

Investing in New Product Development

You must have left out a vital element in the package, an element without which the package does not hold together and all the work is made useless.

That is our response when a manager tells us "we tried that and it did not work."

This entire book is about investing in people, in research, in the whole package which adds up to the innovative company. No part of this package can be safely left out, a fact of which it is hard to convince the impatient executive.

IN AN AGE OF OBSOLESCENCE

Many common, everyday products have demanded huge investments over the past 100 years as a result of technical change. These demands are bound to increase greatly over the next 100 years.

Consider the humble saucepan. No household is without it, but the change from solid fuel hobs and ranges to gas cookers produced a change from the old heavyweights to lighter and cheaper aluminium saucepans which only needed to be capable of standing the flame of the gas burner. A turn back to the saucepan with the more solid bottom matched the emergence of the electric cooker. For most purposes, this meant more solid aluminium products while there was investment also in cast iron saucepans for up-market sales. Innovation in saucepan manufacture was determined by innovation in the heating element on which it sat.

From Flour to Satellites

No household is without flour. Innovation in flour has been influenced by the introduction of bread mixes to cater to the domestic bread-making machine of which sales are gathering pace in the United States and Canada. These sales are sure to increase in Europe as prices come down and will perhaps become a subject for a licensing agreement or other strategic alliance. Manufacturers of plain flours must surely be planning new products to hedge against the threatened obsolescence of much of their existing range. The innovating home-baking device is set to force bakers to rethink their products.

To turn to more sophisticated products, the shift from typewriters to personal computers was a more painful and laborious one. Some manufacturers developed electronic typewriters with small memories to give themselves breathing space. The results were often unsatisfactory, leading to machines which did not perform well and were quickly replaced by the personal computers which have changed with ever-increasing sophistication in a remarkably short time.

Also under the heading of high tech, investment in long-distance cables was overtaken by the invention of optic fibers. One of the present authors can remember the time when the chief executive of a British company with an Australian subsidiary told him how much the long-distance cable had eased his life. Since then it has become possible to dial the Australian management with no more difficulty than the making of a local call, thanks to satellites which made both the wire and the optic fiber communications obsolete. Rumors now abound that the satellites themselves are doomed to become obsolete. If this happens, a huge investment in satellite technology is rendered out of date.

Causes of Obsolescence

At one time, planned obsolescence was widely canvassed among consumer products manufacturers. A contemporary example of planned obsolescence is in razor blades. The Gillette company produces new and improved razors with improved blades to match at regular intervals. This irritates the shaver who expects many years of service out of his existing razor and remembers the days when razors were given away when you bought blades. In spite of this irritation, the company finds that the same shaver comes back for more; Gillette can rely on his satisfaction with the new product. Another element in the armory of the diversifier.

Some of the factors that cause obsolescence are listed in the box "Causes of Obsolescence." Each of the issues in the table must be taken into account when assessing the probable effects of anticipated obsolescence on investment. Most of the issues can be foreseen by a company either through its own direct resources or by sources of intelligence—specialist providers of information, Chambers of Commerce or trade associations—at its disposal. Those "sources of information," which include the Economist Intelligence Unit, the Internet, and the business press, as well as market research companies, are examples of firms in the service industry which need to invest heavily in new product development.

Causes of Obsolescence

1. New environmental legislation
2. Change of fashion
3. Cheaper goods often with improved design from developing and low cost countries, notably those in Southeast Asia
4. More rapid innovation by competitors
5. Changing views on health problems
6. Health and safety regulations
7. The unprecedented speed of innovation, especially in electronics and genetic engineering
8. The discovery of new raw materials

All require special vigilance on the part of responsible managers but numbers (2), (3), and (4) require special attention among consumer products companies, while numbers (1), (5), and (8) are of more immediate interest to capital products manufacturers. Finally, all are of interest to service industries and none can opt out of any.

THE INVESTMENT DECISIONS

Investment begins with a decision on the long-term development program; this is likely to be accompanied by short-term measures, such as planned obsolescence, to keep ahead of competitors. The "long-term" will be fixed by the time horizons of the industry. This ranges from a few months in the most fashion-conscious sectors to twenty-five years in the case of a producer of large complex products such as plane manufacturers.

Budgets for both the long and the short term will include:

- market research
- technical research
- development engineering (updating manuals in the service sector)
- type of plant (whether by flow process or by conversion)
- recruitment and employment of new specialists and technicians
- allowance for slippage
- reduction of profit on existing products or services following the promotion of new ones.

Sources of Funds

If the required funds are provided in the long-term strategic plan and the implementation program, that is a bonus; if not, other options must be considered. One is to identify a business that can reposition the company and raise the funds to buy it. This is ideal if a company is available. A modern approach would be the search for a firm with which it was possible to conclude a form of "strategic alliance" in which two or more companies pool their resources in order to tackle an attractive market. The pooling may be carried out by means of a joint venture, a licensing or franchising agreement, a consortium or a form of subcontracting in which one company undertakes the development work and the other the marketing.

A formal arrangement is required, if both partners are based in industrialized countries, in order to avoid attack under competition legislation (antitrust).

A substantial arrangement in a developing country will usually involve the government which is likely to support the local partner. The part the government plays will be influenced by any perceived advantage to the country if the deal goes through. Assume, however, a suspicion of foreign companies which will complicate negotiations. The foreign firm has to negotiate through a love-hate relationship ("we want you but go away") and needs to prepare for this.

The agreement least likely to receive government approval and most likely to be suitable to company needs is the joint venture in which no new company is incorporated; this has already been mentioned in Chapter 16 without a list of examples because of the delicacy of the subject.

STRATEGIC ALLIANCES

Costly investments may well be funded by a joint venture, a licensing contract, or another arrangement usually known as a strategic alliance. Which type of alliance is chosen will depend on the availability of a partner, the resources required, and the relevant legislation.

These fashionable arrangements appear to be liable to breakdown. The problem is that the sharing, obvious to both parties when embarking on the alliance, is never quite so clear once the activity becomes routine. One partner's contribution is expected to be the marketing but the other partner may well have an ambitious marketing department which will not be sidetracked; at the same time one partner may have agreed to contribute the technical knowledge but is unwilling for the other partner to have the access to patents and other specialized knowledge anticipated when the agreement was put in train. So how are these problems overcome? The box lists some ideas.

Ideas for Overcoming Typical Causes of Disputes in Strategic Alliances

1. *Steering group.* Ensure that the members of any steering group are sufficiently senior and with enough clout to sort out problems.
2. *Policy setting.* Arising from (1), the steering group must have the power to make (or implement) policies which both parties will consider binding.
3. *Performance appraisal.* The steering group must appraise the performance of the alliance with the same strictness as is required of any other activity of each firm.
4. *Contracts.* Contracts are essential to cover any issue over which disputes are thought likely to arise. The contract needs to propose an arbitrator in case of a failure to agree. The very nature of international business means that the arbitrator will not be a national of one partner; arbitration will normally take place in the country and subject to the laws of the dominant company—but every possible provision should be undertaken to prevent disputes reaching the point where an arbitrator is needed.
5. *Scale of operations.* The scale of the operations needs to be determined beforehand and enshrined in the contracts.
6. *Who does what?* This needs to be stipulated in the contract.

Failing the possibility of generating funds through the long-term plans or of entering a takeover or a strategic alliance, other possibilities include streamlining the business to increase the profitability to pay for the innovation program; this would involve eliminating low profit products or services.

Examples

Recent examples of firms that have gone down one or other of the routes available for financing new product developments include:

- *The merger.* A hand tool company needing to supply power tools purchased an existing power tool manufacturer with an excellent product but indifferent marketing. This saved the huge costs needed to start from scratch.
- *The consortium.* This is used in large projects. For instance, several large European firms have been involved in researching, developing, and manufacturing the European Airbus. Banks seeking to finance major capital projects in developing countries often seek to protect themselves by forming a consortium; this also gives their bid more credibility.
- *Subcontracting.* A large, British producer of industrial ceramics runs a research and development department specializing in adhesives. This came into existence as a result of a massive contract in the United States some years earlier. The contract featured a significant adhesive factor. At the conclusion of the contract, the company placed the department at the disposal of an adhesive manufacturer either to "hire" it or to acquire it.

Never forget that there are huge opportunities for subcontracting in even the largest of contracts. The small- and medium-sized concern (the SME) can find plenty of opportunities in products (like airplanes) that are outside their reach. The Boeing purchasing manual is an enormous volume, not a slim pocket book. Included are ashtrays, lightbulbs, and seat covers as well as jet nozzles. The challenge to the small company is to find a product or component robust enough for the customer.

In addition to business cooperation agreements ("strategic alliances"), there are a range of grants to be obtained varying from local government subsidies to a loan from the European Union. Development funding may also be possible in appropriate circumstances.

The Investment Appraisal

Once the investment is seen to be necessary, the company's planners will check it through their normal investment appraisal procedures to ensure that it fits the criteria for return on investment over the anticipated lifetime of the product. As with all such procedures which depend on forecasts, the results need to be read with scepticism to allow for over-optimistic projections. Will the market really develop over the timescale in the manner assumed? A doubtful response may well be held to be a negative on the whole procedure—it is saying: "think again."

What Have We Learned from This Chapter?

- The need for investment frequently arises from obsolescence (the causes of which are listed in the box on p. 197).
- The costs of investment which will determine the investment decision are presented in budgets for the long- and short-term requirements. These include direct costs such as research and development engineering, along with indirect costs such as the recruitment of new staff and allowances for slippage and the reduction of profits anticipated from the products or services made obsolete.

Chapter 19

The Product Launch:
Looking Ahead, Some Ethical Issues

The CEO of IBM, Louis V. Gerstner Jr., was widely quoted in the press when faced with the challenge of turning around the beleaguered computer maker, "The last thing IBM requires right now is a vision."

Michael E. Raynor

When preparing a first draft of this chapter, the attention of one of the authors was caught by the above quotation at the start of an article intriguingly titled "That vision thing. Do we need it?" by a doctoral candidate at the Harvard Business School. What Mr. Gerstner Jr. would repudiate if anyone was bold enough to tell him was that he had a vision for IBM and—surprise, surprise—it worked. The vision was that a short period of patience was needed to reorient a company with enormous resources and operations in a rapidly growing market.

The quoted article analyzed vague terms such as "mission" and "vision" and took their meanings back to their commercial origins in "core competencies," "values," and "market forces." We like to think that this is what we have done in this book, perhaps to excess. In this chapter new product development is examined in the light of all the factors that might influence it beginning with Part I, which outlined in some detail the physical (resources available) and psychological (pressure for speedy and well-informed action) factors required in the search for new products. This theme was developed and expanded in Part II when the sources and uses of ideas (Chapter 5) were explored in the context of the issues that make for success including Chapter 6 on the strategy linking resource input to profit output. Then Part III looked at "centers of excellence," first of all in their own right and as points of focus in other influences on innovation such as: staffing, subcontracting, design, technical research and high-tech products, market research, and relations between companies and governments. This Part also looks at the special problems of basic industries pointing out these (agriculture, coal, metals) have had many years' experience of diversification but a more active partnership with scientific and technical research is needed if the diversification is ever to begin to support the populations previously living off the basic industries.

So we come to the great day when marketing department executives are busy putting into practice the long-planned launch. A dynamic, thrusting firm which is launching a series of new products will need to work out guidelines to determine who will be called upon to be present at a particular launch. These will vary from the chief executive plus a celebrity from outside the company if the product is particularly novel or important. At the next level of importance, a raft of senior executives will be summoned to appear and so on down to a modest and mundane variation on an existing product. For this only the manager of the team that worked out the innovation will appear along with the head of the department which will be using the new product. If the business is in a sector currently in the news, such as public transport, although this is being written at the beginning of the twenty-first century, representatives of transport users and local authorities may be called upon to be present. Simultaneous launches in different parts of a country will take place whether the new initiative is in bus or rail facilities or even a new road.

THE PRODUCT LAUNCH

This is the crucial activity, promotion. How can would-be customers actually buy the goods or services unless their existence is known to them? One of the problems about publicity is that the development of the product often must be kept secret for fear that a competitor will get wind of what is happening and launch first. There are circumstances where it is best not to be first in; these mainly occur for new products which are also novel and require a measure of market preparation; for most new products, which are a development from an established product or service, the secrecy is not needed so much as speed to market, while (as the saying goes) all publicity is good publicity and the company cannot afford to lose any chance to become better known, even if that increases the risk of defeat by a competitor.

New product development is always risky and raises the question: Will the new product make profits that are an adequate return on the total investment (time, money, and reputation) placed in it? We have already proposed that each project must be costed so that the possible losses are within the company's finite resources: it must, in other words, run its own insurance policy against a failure. This must be done without killing enthusiasm within the firm.

Within the limits just described, it is important to leak news of the launch at the earliest safe moment. By this means the actual launch is anticipated and customers will be alerted that the product is soon to be available.

Let us assume that there are two kinds of new product: the novelty or striking development designed to be a market winner, and the less-significant development of an existing product. A product cannot be expected to fit neatly into one category or the other. It may not be a striking novelty or a minor development, but will often be a combination of the two. Let us take an example from the bus industry.

The change from a weekly bus service to a daily is a change of product for villages which have only had the weekly provision before. For those villages the change is a major one, meriting a top-level launch, even though for most of the country regular daily services are the norm. The planning of the change will include information about the potential number of passengers available and the frequency of their journeys; it will also include information about the total marketing package required to persuade the potential customers actually to use the buses as well as the availability of cars in the area. Policymakers may like to note that where the potential market is small, competition does not benefit the consumer. In the case of transport this means that no operator can see any benefit in cutting prices only to add to the loss-making, which a small increase in customers will not avoid.

These studies will result in some return on investment calculations to see if the daily services can be commercially viable. If they cannot, then a search will have to be made for sources of subsidy such as local authorities or big employers on the route. The subsidizers will expect their payback in substantial publicity, including an honored place at the launch. Their conditions will have to be included in the plans. Many uneconomic rail services in Britain are already reviewed by user groups which might be used to raise funds for specific projects such as station improvements. For transport services, both bus and rail, there is a chance of a one-off subsidy from a charitable trust responding to an appeal for a center of population that found itself cut off from public transport. But a village of 300 inhabitants cannot be expected to support its own daily public transport even if there is commuter traffic to be won; this means using ingenuity to place this village on a route that includes others or running excursions to tourist scenes in the place. Of course, the building of an area of new housing in or near the village is likely to change the situation completely and a watch on local plans will be needed. Similarly shops, banks, and perhaps pubs will have closed in the light of limited usage and a public transport enterprise will not contribute to their reopening; on the other hand, the reopened facilities might be inclined to subsidize the public transport as might the county council. Cross-subsidization of enterprises which depend upon one another has already been seen and may well increase.

ETHICAL ISSUES

We promised in Chapter 1 to consider ethical issues later. The number one ethical issue is the subject just discussed of subsidy. It is often alleged that subsidizing public transport is using money from local or state taxes levied on the homes of manual workers to give assistance to richer managers and office workers. To this the authorities reply that the purpose of the subsidy is to reduce congestion and pollution which damages the lives of all householders in urban areas whatever their occupation.

Local authorities subsidize facilities for pedestrians and cyclists for a similar reason—to improve health.

To change the subject, we talk of "exploiting a market" but, realistically, a market is a group of people and the word "exploiting" has two different meanings: first, the sense in which we usually employ the word, is "making use of"—entering a market; the other is making use of sophisticated techniques to persuade people to buy products they neither need nor want. So "exploiting" becomes an ethical issue if there is any suspicion of overpersuading people into buying products that are either harmful, unnecessary, or both. Any form of overpersuasion might be considered immoral and this is always a danger when launching new products.

It has been argued that there are no ethical issues in new product development, only in its promotion and use. In these days of ethical investment, that must be questioned; in any case there are some products that most people would consider unworthy of development in a civilized country, such as implements for torture or execution, and diversification into these must be considered unethical—at least in terms of twenty-first century outlooks. That last clause is a necessary reminder that ethics are not timeless but relative to the outlook of the age. There stands a factory on the outskirts of Manchester (England) that was built to make chains for slaves. It has undergone many diversifications since, but its original product would be considered unethical today whatever view was taken in its time and however much demand there might be for the product.

Many organizations exist nowadays to promote what they call "ethical investment." The products excluded vary from organization to organization. Sometimes it is the product that is excluded, such as armaments and cigarettes; sometimes it is the production process such as sports clothes made by child labor in developing countries. In either case—the product or the process—the ethical issue is a subtle one; it is never absolute. Child labor may be an inescapable stage in the progress toward industrialization. If so, it is hypocritical for people from countries that are already industrialized to condemn it.

If you have any doubt about new product development raising ethical issues, imagine insurance companies diversifying into the investigation of genes. Some of these companies are probably doing this now. We cannot rehearse the arguments here, but few people would doubt that there are ethical issues, both for and against.

Another issue is writing off a whole population on the assumption that their needs cannot be met economically. Unilever blew up this assumption as a result of their special market research in Brazil (see Chapter 15). Both company and consumer may be thought to benefit by such widening of horizons.

Cigarettes were mentioned in Chapter 1 and their sale in developing countries has been represented on the one hand as offering people a "wider choice" in countries where the number of people who can afford them is gradually increasing, to the point where they make a worthwhile market. This outlook is opposed by those who consider a policy of promoting tobacco among those who can only just afford it as "brainwashing." The same argument is used against the sale of formula milk in some developing countries. People who have not been subjected to advanced methods of promotion for generations may find the methods used hard to resist. The argument over formula milk, which may under certain circumstances be a necessity, is even more subtle than that over tobacco which is only considered a luxury.

The simple criterion for considering ethical issues in new product development is in answering the question: Will this product bring benefit or harm in terms of current civilized outlooks? If "harm," don't touch it.

Not the Whole Story

We have touched lightly on the subject of how business ethics affect new product development, just trying to bring out a limited range of relevant issues from a vast subject; this has been our approach all through the book. However, the subject of business ethics must be touched on lightly otherwise it is truly the subject for another book.

References

Barro, Robert J. (1998). "Why the anti-trust cops should lay off high tech." *Business Week,* August 17, p. 40.

Chisnall, P.M. (1992). *Marketing Research,* Fourth Edition. London: McGraw-Hill.

Department of International Development (1997). *Eliminating World Poverty.* London: Stationery Office Ltd.

Gort, P. (1990). *Design Management: Papers from the London Business School.* London: Architectural Design and Technology.

"Indian success is a model for the region." (1998). *Financial Times,* July 1.

Institute of Personnel and Development (1999). *Contract of Employment.* Britain: Author.

"It's simply obvious companies live by innovation alone." *The Observer,* Business Supplement, June 28, 1998, London.

Lacey, Robert (1981). *The Kingdom.* London: Hutchinson.

Lewis, Jim (1999). *London's Lea Valley.* London: Historical Publications.

"Poor Mr. Gates." (1997). *The Economist,* July 26.

"R and D is not an end, but no R and D is the beginning of the end." *The Observer,* June 28, 1998, London.

Raynor, Michael E. "That vision thing. Do we need it?"

"Safe climate, sound business. Action agenda for the private sector." *Business North West,* December 1997, p. 30.

Index of Names

Index of Topics

This index is designed to help readers find their way to the main topics considered in this book. Only references to pages that have significant information are included.